365 DAYꜱ ᴏᴦ MEDITATIONS

FROM DIOGENES THE CYNIC

&

ARISTIPPUS THE CYRENAIC

Editor: Frances Roseuvir, 2020

Printed in the United States of America.

INTRODUCTION

The purpose of this book is simple – provide daily meditations from Diogenes the Cynic and Aristippus the Cyrenaic.

These two figures encapsulate the best of Greek philosophy as a way of life. Although Diogenes and Aristippus approach philosophy from different angles, they are both on the same spectrum. They were seeking to challenge peoples' ideas about what constitutes the "good life", to think hard about our ethical selves, and to challenge core beliefs..

The book is structured in a simple manner. It follows the form of a devotional in that there is a daily reading meant for reflection. In terms of size, I have compressed the information into the smallest book possible to keep the cost to a minimum and the portability to the maximum.

SOURCES

Aelian – *Varia Historia* | Aelianus, Claudius.
Claudius Ælianus, His Various History. Translated
by T. Stanley, Thomas Dring, 1666.

Aesop | Aesop. *Aesop's Fables*. Translated by L.
Gibbs, OUP Oxford, 2008.

Antiphilus of Byzantium – On Diogenes | Paton,
R., translator. *The Greek Anthology: With an English
Translation by William R. Paton*. In 5 Volumes. W.
Heinemann, G. P. Putnam's Sons, 1916.

Apuleius – Florida | Apuleius. *The Apologia and
Florida of Apuleius of Madaura*. Translated by H.E.
Butler, Clarendon Press, 1909.

Aristotle – Rhetoric | Aristotle. *The Rhetoric of
Aristotle: Collection of Pamphlets on Aristotle*. 1936.

Athenaeus – Deipnosophistae | Athenaeus. *The
Deipnosophists; Or, Banquet of the Learned*. Translated
by C.D. Yonge, H.G. Bohn, 1854.

Augustine – City of God | Schaff, P., and H.
Wace, editors. *A Select Library of Nicene and Post-
Nicene Fathers of the Christian Church*. 1895. Christian
literature Company, 1895.

Aulus Gellius – Attic Nights | Gellius, A. *The
Attic Nights*. Translated by J.C. Rolfe, Harvard
University Press, 1927.

Basil of Caesarea – Letters | Schaff, P., and H. Wace, editors. *A Select Library of Nicene and Post-Nicene Fathers of the Christian Church*. 1895. Christian literature Company, 1895.

Cicero – Tusculan Disputations | Cicero, M. T. Cicero's Tusculan Disputations: Also Treatises *On the Nature of the Gods, and On the Commonwealth*. Translated by C.D. Yonge, Harper & Brothers, 1877.

Clement of Alexandria – Pedagogy | Roberts, A., et al., editors. *The Ante-Nicene Fathers: Translations of the Writings of the Fathers down to A.D. 325*. C. Scribner's sons, 1906.

Clement – Stromata | Roberts, A., et al., editors. *The Ante-Nicene Fathers: Translations of the Writings of the Fathers down to A.D. 325*. C. Scribner's sons, 1906.

Demetrius – On Style | Demetrius. Demetrius *On Style: The Greek Text of Demetrius De Elocutione*. Translated by W.R. Roberts, University Press, 1902.

Dio Chrysostom – Discourses | Chyrosotom, Dio. Dio Chrysostom, *Discourses*. Translated by J.W. Cohoon and H.L. Crosby, W. Heinemann, Limited, 1932.

Diogenes Laertius – Lives | Laertius, D. *The Lives and Opinions of Eminent Philosophers. Translated by C.D. Yonge*. London: Henry G. Bohn, 1853

Epictetus – Discourses | Epictetus. *The Discourses
and Manual: Together with Fragments of His Writings.*
Translated by P.E. Matheson, Clarendon Press,
1916.

Greek Anthology | Paton, R., translator. *The Greek
Anthology: With an English Translation by William R.
Paton. In 5 Volumes.* W. Heinemann, G. P.
Putnam's Sons, 1916.

Jerome – Against Jovinian | Schaff, P., and H.
Wace, editors. *A Select Library of Nicene and Post-
Nicene Fathers of the Christian Church.* 1895. Christian
literature Company, 1895.

Julian – Orations | Julian the Emperor. *Works of
Julian the Emperor.* Heinemann, 1913.

Juvenal – Satires | Ramsay, G. G., and Juvenal,
translators. *Juvenal and Persius.* W. Heinemann,
1918.

Lucian – Expositions | Samosata, Lucian of, et al.
*The Works of Lucian of Samosata: Complete with
Exceptions Specified in the Preface.* Clarendon Press,
1905.

Marcus Aurelius | Aurelius, Marcus. *The Thoughts
of the Emperor Marcus Aurelius Antoninus.* Translated
by G. Long, Little, Brown, 1897.

Pausanias – Description of Greece | Pausanias.
Pausanias *Description of Greece.* Translated by
W.H.S. Jones et al., W. Heinemann, 1918.

Philo – Every Good Man is Free | Philo Judaeus. *Works of Philo*: Translated from the Greek by C. D. Yonge. H. G. Bohn, 1854.

Philostratus – Life of Apollonius | Philostratus the Younger. *The Life of Apollonius of Tyana: The Epistles of Apollonius and the Treatise of Eusebius.* Translated by F.C. Conybeare, William Heinemann, 1912.

Plutarch – Lives | Plutarch. *Plutarch's Lives: The Translation Called Dryden's.* Translated by J. Dryden and A.H. Clough, Little, Brown and company, 1888.

Plutarch – Essays | Plutarch. *Plutarch's Morals, Tr. by Several Hands. Corrected and Revised by W.W. Goodwin.* Edited by W.W. Goodwin, 1874.

Seneca – Essays | Seneca. Seneca: *Moral Essays.* Translated by J.W. Basore et al., Harvard Unviersity Press, 1917.

Seneca – Epistles | Seneca, L. A. Seneca: *Epistles 1-65.* Translated by R.M. Gummere, Harvard University Press, 1917.

Socrates Scholasticus | Schaff, P., and H. Wace, editors. *A Select Library of Nicene and Post-Nicene Fathers of the Christian Church.* 1895. Christian literature Company, 1895.

Strabo – Geography | Strabo. *The Geography of Strabo.* George Bell & Sons, 1903.

Suda | "Aristippus." *Suda On Line*. Tr. Jennifer
Benedict. 31 March 2002. 15 November 2015.
<http://www.stoa.org/sol-entries/alpha/3909>.

Tertullian – Ad Nationes | Roberts, A., et al.,
editors. *The Ante-Nicene Fathers: Translations of the
Writings of the Fathers down to A.D. 325*. C.
Scribner's sons, 1906.

Theophilus – Letter to Autolycus | Roberts, A., et
al., editors. *The Ante-Nicene Fathers: Translations of
the Writings of the Fathers down to A.D. 325*. C.
Scribner's sons, 1906.

Vitruvius – On Architecture | Vitruvius Pollio;
Morris Hicky Morgan, Ed. *Books on Architecture*.
Morris Hicky Morgan, Ed. Harvard University
Press: 1914.

TABLE OF CONTENTS

JANUARY

365 Days of Meditations from Diogenes the Cynic and Aristippus the Cyrenaic

---

JANUARY 1

Diogenes Laertius – Book 6.3

When [Diogenes] had written to someone to look out and get ready a small house for him, as he delayed to do it, he took a [jar] which he found in the Temple of Cybele[1], for his house.

JANUARY 2

Diogenes Laertius – Book 6.43

Dionysius the Stoic, says that after the Battle of Chaeronea[2] [Diogenes] was taken prisoner and brought to Philip; and being asked who he was replied, "A spy, to spy upon your insatiability." And Philip marveled at him and let him go.

JANUARY 3

Plutarch – Consolation to Apollonius 12

Diogenes the Cynic, when a little before his death he fell into a slumber, and his physician rousing him out of it asked him whether anything ailed

---

[1] Cybele is equivalent to "the great mother" and considered a protector. Her temple, also called the Metroum, was on the hillside below the Parthenon.

[2] Battle of Chaeronea was the final victory of Macedon over Greece, and established hegemony in Southern Greece. It took place on August 2, 338 BCE.

him, wisely answered, "Nothing, sir, only one brother anticipates another — Sleep before Death"[3].

JANUARY 4

Diogenes Laertius – Book 6.39

A [wasteful] eunuch had written on his house, "Let no evil thing enter in." "Where," said Diogenes, "is the master of the house going?"

JANUARY 5

Diogenes Laertius – Book 6.63

He used to say that courtesans were the queens of kings; for [the courtesans] asked [the kings] for whatever they chose.

JANUARY 6

Diogenes Laertius – Book 6.50

When he was asked how Dionysius[4] treats his friends, he said, "Like bags; those which are full he hangs up, and those which are empty he throws away."

---

[3] Hypnos (Sleep) was the brother of Thanatos (Death).
[4] Dionysius II of Syracuse

JANUARY 7

Julian – Oration 6

Moreover [any random cynic] even ridicules the
eating of octopus and says that Diogenes paid a
sufficient penalty for his folly and vanity in that he
perished of this diet as though by a draught of
hemlock.

JANUARY 8

Diogenes Laertius – Book 6.59

[Diogenes] used to say that men were wrong for
complaining of fortune; for that they ask of the
Gods what appear to be good things, not what are
really so.

JANUARY 9

Diogenes Laertius – Book 6.66

Being reproached with drinking in a tavern,
"Well," said [Diogenes], "I also get my hair cut in
a barber's shop."

JANUARY 10

Diogenes Laertius – Book 6.37

For [according to Diogenes]: everything belongs
to the Gods; and the Gods are friends to the wise;

and all the property of friends is held in common; therefore everything belong to the wise.

JANUARY 11

Diogenes Laertius – Book 2.68

Being asked what [Diogenes] had gained from philosophy, he replied, "The ability to feel at ease in any society."

JANUARY 12

Diogenes Laertius – Book 6.65

To a man who treated his father with contempt, [Diogenes] said, "Are you not ashamed to despise him to whom you owe it that you have it in your power to give yourself airs at all?"

JANUARY 13

Diogenes Laertius – Book 6.67

[Diogenes] once asked an [spendthrift] fellow for a mina[5]; and when he put the question to him, why he asked others for an obol, and him for a mina, he said, "Because I hope to get something from the others another time, but the Gods alone

---

[5] 1 Mina = Approx. 420 Obols

know whether I shall ever extract anything from
you again."

Diogenes Laertius – Book 6.67

One day [Diogenes] saw an unskillful archer
shooting; so he went and sat down by the target,
saying, "Now I shall be out of harm's way."

Diogenes Laertius – Book 6.26

On one occasion Plato had invited some friends
who had come to him from Dionysius to a
banquet, and Diogenes trampled on his carpets,
and said, "Thus I trample on the empty pride of
Plato;" and Plato made him answer, "How much
arrogance are you displaying, Diogenes! when you
think that you are not arrogant at all."

Diogenes Laertius – Book 6.14

Once [Diogenes] saw a youth studying
philosophy, and said to him, "Well done;
inasmuch as you are leading those who admire
your person to contemplate the beauty of your
mind."

JANUARY 17

Diogenes Laertius – Book 6.54

On one occasion, [Diogenes] was asked by a
certain person, "What sort of a man, O Diogenes,
do you think Socrates?" and he said, "A
madman."

JANUARY 18

Diogenes Laertius – Book 6.51

When [Diogenes] was asked what was miserable in
life, he answered, "An indigent old man."

JANUARY 19

Diogenes Laertius – Book 6.51

When the question was put to [Diogenes], what
beast inflicts the worst bite, he said, "Of wild
beasts the sycophant, and of tame animals the
flatterer."

JANUARY 20

Diogenes Laertius – Book 6.45

At another time, seeing a young man throwing
stones at the gallows, [Diogenes] said, "Well done,
you will be sure to reach the mark."

JANUARY 21

Diogenes Laertius – Book 6.29

When [Diogenes] was ordered not to sit down; "It makes no difference," said he, "for fish are sold, wherever they are found."

JANUARY 22

Diogenes Laertius – Book 6.46

On one occasion, when a youth was playing the kottabus[6] in the bath, [Diogenes] said to him, "The better you do it, the worse you do it."

JANUARY 23

Aesop 58 – Diogenes and the Bald Man

A bald man insulted Diogenes the Cynic, and Diogenes replied, "Far be it from me to make insults! But I do want to compliment your hair for having abandoned such a worthless head."

JANUARY 24

Diogenes Laertius – Book 6.45

---

[6] A game played at ancient Greek drinking parties. The game is played by flinging wine lees (sediment) at targets. The player would utter the name of the object of his affection.

On one occasion, when he had seen the hieromnemones[7] leading off one of the stewards who had stolen a goblet, he said, "The great thieves are carrying off the little thief."

JANUARY 25

Dio Chrysostom – The Eighth Discourse – On Virtue

Antisthenes tolerated this banter of [Diogenes] since he greatly admired the man's character; and so, in [return] for being called a trumpet, he used to say that Diogenes was like the wasps, the buzz of whose wings is slight but the sting very sharp.

JANUARY 26

Aelian – Varia Historia 9.28 – Of Diogenes

A Spartan commending this Verse of Hesiod:

Not even an Ox would die,
Unless the neighbour is bad

…and Diogenes hearing him, "But, said he, the Messenians[8] and their Oxen were destroyed, and you are their Neighbours."

JANUARY 27

---

[7] Custodians of state papers and recorders of judicial decisions.
[8] The Messenians were subjugated by the Spartans.

Diogenes Laertius – Book 6.51

[Diogenes] called the belly, the Charybdis of life.

JANUARY 28

Philo – Every Good Man is Free 121-126

And then, when [Diogenes] had obtained
sufficient food, and when he was about to be sold
with the rest of the captives, he sat down first, and
breakfasted with great cheerfulness and courage,
giving some of his breakfast to his neighbours.

JANUARY 29

Dio Chrysostom – The Sixth Discourse –
Diogenes, or On Tyranny

In fact, Diogenes was not neglectful of his body as
certain foolish people thought; but when they saw
him often shivering and living in the open and
going thirsty, they imagined that he was careless of
his health and life, whereas this rigorous regime
gave him better health than fell to the lot of those
who were ever gorging themselves, better than fell
to the lot of those who stayed indoors and never
experienced either cold or heat.

JANUARY 30

Lucian – Dialogues of the Dead 13

Diogenes. Dear me, Alexander, are you dead like
the rest of us?

Alexander. As you see, sir; is there anything
extraordinary in a mortal's dying?

Diogenes. So Ammon[9] lied when he said you were
his son; you were Philip's after all.

JANUARY 31

Diogenes Laertius – Book 6.54

When asked what [Diogenes] would take to let a
man give him a blow on the head? He replied, "A
helmet."

---

[9] Egyptian equivalent of Zeus

FEBRUARY

FEBRUARY 1

Diogenes Laertius – Book 6.57

On one occasion, [Diogenes] met Anaximenes,
the orator, who was a fat man, and thus
confronted him; "Pray give us, who are poor,
some of your belly; for by so doing you will be
relieved yourself, and you will assist us."

FEBRUARY 2

Diogenes Laertius – Book 6.32

Once, [Diogenes] called out, "Holloa, men." And
when some people gathered round him in
consequence he drove them away with his stick,
saying, "I called men, and not dregs."

FEBRUARY 3

Diogenes Laertius – Book 6.57

Once, when he was discussing some point,
Diogenes held up a piece of salt fish, and drew off
the attention of his hearers; and as Anaximenes
was indignant at this, he said, "see, one
pennyworth of salt fish has put an end to the
lecture of Anaximenes."

FEBRUARY 4

Diogenes Laertius – Book 6.27

On one occasion, when no one came to listen to
[Diogenes] while he was discoursing seriously, he
began to whistle. And then when people flocked
round him, he reproached them for coming with
eagerness to folly, but being lazy and indifferent
about good things.

FEBRUARY 5

Plutarch – Whether Water or Fire Be Most Useful
2

That this is no poetical fiction is demonstrable
from this, that there are many sorts of people that
live without fire, without houses, and without
hearths, in the open air. And Diogenes the Cynic
made no use of fire; so that after he had
swallowed a raw fish, "This hazard," said he, "do I
run for your sakes." But without water no man
ever thought it convenient or possible to live.

FEBRUARY 6

Diogenes Laertius – Book 6.60

Once Alexander the Great came and stood by
him, and said, "I am Alexander, the great king."
"And I," said he, "am Diogenes the dog."

FEBRUARY 7

Basil of Caesarea – Letter 4

Diogenes, who prided himself on requiring no
more than was absolutely necessary, flung away
his bowl after he had learned from some lad to
stoop down and drink from the hollow of his
hand

FEBRUARY 8

Diogenes Laertius – Book 6.72

And [Diogenes] played in the same manner with
the topics of noble birth, and reputation, and all
things of that kind, saying that they were all veils,
as it were, for wickedness.

FEBRUARY 9

Diogenes Laertius – Book 6.55

Being asked what kind of hound he was, he
replied, "When hungry, a Maltese[10]; when full, a
Molossian[11] – two breeds which most people
praise, though for fear of fatigue they do not
venture out hunting with them. So neither can you

---

[10] The Maltese dog was a lapdog (toy dog) favored by both the
ancient Greeks and Romans, especially their children
[11] Aristotle in his *History of Animals* wrote "In the Molossian race of
dogs, those employed in hunting differ in no respect from other
dogs; while those employed in following sheep are larger and more
fierce in their attack on wild beasts."

live with me, because you are afraid of the discomforts."

FEBRUARY 10

Diogenes Laertius – Book 6.73

Music and geometry, and astronomy, and all things of that kind, he neglected, as useless and unnecessary. But he was a man very happy in meeting arguments.

FEBRUARY 11

Diogenes Laertius – Book 6.24

[Diogenes] used likewise to say, "that when in the course of his life he beheld pilots, and physicians, and philosophers, he thought man the wisest of all animals; but when again he beheld interpreters of dreams, and soothsayers, and those who listened to them, and men puffed up with glory or riches, then he thought that there was not a more foolish animal than man."

FEBRUARY 12

Diogenes Laertius – Book 6.79

But some say that when dying he left instructions that they should throw him out unburied, that every wild beast might feed on him, or thrust him into a ditch and sprinkle a little dust over him. But

according to others his instructions were that they
should throw him into the Ilissus, in order that he
might be useful to his brethren.

FEBRUARY 13

Lucian – The Way to Write History 3

[When Philip[12] was invading Corinth], Diogenes
having nothing to do — of course no one thought
of giving him a job — was moved by the sight to
gird up his philosopher's cloak and begin rolling
his tub-dwelling energetically up and down the
Craneum; an acquaintance asked, and got, the
explanation: "I do not want to be thought the only
idler in such a busy multitude; I am rolling my tub
to be like the rest."

FEBRUARY 14

Aulus Gellius – Attic Nights 2.18

Diogenes the Cynic also served as a slave, but he
was a freeborn man, who was sold into slavery.
When Xeniades of Corinth wished to buy him and
asked whether he knew any trade, Diogenes
replied: "I know how to govern free men." Then
Xeniades, in admiration of his answer, bought
him, set him free, and entrusting to him his own
children, said: "Take my children to govern."

---

[12] Father of Alexander the Great, conqueror of Greece

FEBRUARY 15

Plutarch – That Virtue May Be Taught

Diogenes, seeing a youth devouring his [food and drink] too greedily, gave his tutor a box on the ear, and that deservedly, as judging it the fault of him that had not taught, not of him that had not learned better manners.

FEBRUARY 16

Demetrius – On Style 261-262

So also with his words to the handsome youth, when wrestling with whom Diogenes unawares assumed an unseemly position. The lad was frightened and started back. "Never fear, my dear boy," he exclaimed, "I am not your match in that way."

FEBRUARY 17

Diogenes Laertius – Book 6.60

And when [Diogenes] was asked to what actions of his it was owing that he was called a dog, he said, "Because I fawn upon those who give me anything, and bark at those who give me nothing, and bite the rogues."

FEBRUARY 18

Diogenes Laertius – Book 6.51

[Diogenes] used to say that a speech, the object of which was solely to please, was a honeyed [tether].

FEBRUARY 19

Diogenes Laertius – Book 6.43

Once, at the Olympic Games when the herald proclaimed "Dioxippus[13] is the conqueror of men;" [Diogenes] said, "He is the conqueror of slaves, I am the conqueror of men."

FEBRUARY 20

Diogenes Laertius – Book 6.72

[Diogenes] said, that all people's sons ought to belong to everyone in common.

FEBRUARY 21

Diogenes Laertius – Book 6.49

Once [Diogenes] saw a man who had been victor at the Olympic games, feeding (nemonta) sheep, and he said to him, "You have soon come across

---

[13] Renowned for his Olympic victories at pankration, a sport that combined wrestling and boxing and literally meant "all force"

my friend from the Olympic Games, to the
Nemean[14]."

FEBRUARY 22

Marcus Aurelius – Book 8.3

Alexander and Caius and Pompeius, what are they
in comparison with Diogenes and Heraclitus and
Socrates[15]? For they were acquainted with things,
and their causes [forms], and their matter, and the
ruling principles of these men were the same [or
conformable to their pursuits]. But as to the
others, how many things had they to care for, and
to how many things were they slaves!

FEBRUARY 23

Diogenes Laertius – Book 6.51

On one occasion [Diogenes] saw two Centaurs
very badly painted; he said, "Which of the two is
the worst?"

FEBRUARY 24

Diogenes Laertius – Book 6.32

Once, when a man had conducted [Diogenes] into

---

[14] One of the four Panhellenic Games, similar to the Olympic Games
[15] Generals and leaders versus philosophers

a magnificent house, and had told him that he
must not spit, after hawking a little, he spit in his
face, saying that he could not find a worse place.
But some tell this story of Aristippus.

FEBRUARY 25

Diogenes Laertius – Book 6.76

Cercidas[16] speaks thus of him in his *Meliambics*:

He, that Sinopian [Diogenes] who bore the stick,
Wore his cloak doubled, and in th" open air
Dined without washing, would not bear with life
A moment longer: but he shut his teeth,
And held his breath. He truly was the son
Of Zeus, and a most heavenly-minded dog,
The wise Diogenes.

FEBRUARY 26

Diogenes Laertius – Book 6.39

When a man was talking about the heavenly
bodies and meteors, "Pray how many days," said
[Diogenes] to him, "is it since you came down
from heaven?"

FEBRUARY 27

---

[16] A Cynic philosopher-poet

Diogenes Laertius – Book 6.70

[Diogenes] used to allege as proofs of this, and of the ease which practice imparts to acts of virtue, that people could see that in the case of mere common working trades, and other employments of that kind, the artisans arrived at no inconsiderable accuracy by constant practice; and that any one may see how much one flute player, or one wrestler, is superior to another, by his own continued practice.

FEBRUARY 28

Diogenes Laertius – Book 6.59

[Diogenes] was on one occasion returning from Lacedaemon[17] to Athens; and when someone asked him, "Whither are you going, and whence do you come?" he said, "I am going from the men's apartments to the women's."

FEBRUARY 29

---

[17] Lacedaemon is the region where Sparta is located

MARCH

MARCH 1

Diogenes Laertius – Book 6.33

[Diogenes] used to say that he was the hound of
those who were praised; but that none of those
who praised him dared to go out hunting with
him.

MARCH 2

Diogenes Laertius – Book 6.24

Another of [Diogenes] sayings was, "that he
thought a man ought oftener to provide himself
with a reason than with a collar."

MARCH 3

Diogenes Laertius – Book 6.48

When a young man was one day making a display
of himself, he, having filled the bosom of his robe
with lupins (or beans), began to eat them; and
when the multitude looked at him, [Diogenes]
said, "that he marvelled at their leaving the young
man to look at him."

MARCH 4

Plutarch – How a Man May Receive Advantage
and Profit from his Enemies

And here may be inserted that wise and facetious answer of Diogenes to one that asked him how he might be revenged of his enemy: The only way, says he, to gall and fret him effectually is for yourself to appear a good and honest man.

MARCH 5

Diogenes Laertius – Book 6.54

A man said to him one day, "Many people laugh at you." "But I," [Diogenes] replied, "am not laughed down."

MARCH 6

Diogenes Laertius – Book 6.62

On one occasion [Diogenes] saw the son of a courtesan throwing a stone at a crowd, and said to him, "Take care, lest you hit your father."

MARCH 7

Philo – Every Good Man is Free 157

Accordingly Diogenes said, "It is just as if any one were to proclaim, that some one of his servants was, from this day forth, to be accounted a good grammarian, or geometrician, or musician, without his having the very slightest idea of the art; for just as the proclamation would not make men learned, so also it would not make them free (for then it

would be a blessed thing), but all that it could do
would be to make them no longer slaves."

MARCH 8

Diogenes Laertius – Book 6.73

[Diogenes] said, [...] there was nothing intolerable
in the idea of taking anything out of a temple, or
eating any animal whatever, and that there was no
impiety in tasting even human flesh; as is plain
from the habits of foreign nations; and [Diogenes]
said that this principle might be correctly extended
to every case and every people.

MARCH 9

Diogenes Laertius – Book 6.31-32

And the same author affirms, that [Diogenes]
grew old in the household of Xeniades[18], and that
when he died he was buried by his sons. And that
while he was living with him, Xeniades once asked
him how he should bury him; and he said, "On
my face;" and when he was asked why, he said,
"Because, in a little while, everything will be
turned upside down." And he said this because
the Macedonians were already attaining power,
and becoming a mighty people from having been
very inconsiderable.

---

[18] According to legend, Xeniades purchased Diogenes as a slave after
Diogenes was captured by pirates

MARCH 10

Diogenes Laertius – Book 6.42

When Lysias, the drug-seller, asked [Diogenes]
whether he thought that there are any Gods:
"How," said he, "can I help thinking so, when I
consider you to be hated by them?" but some
attribute this reply to Theodorus[19].

MARCH 11

Diogenes Laertius – Book 6.61

One of [Diogenes'] sayings was, that good-looking
courtesans were like poisoned mead.

MARCH 12

Diogenes Laertius – Book 6.53

And [Diogenes] addressed a man who was buying
delicacies at a great expense: Not long, my son,
will you on earth remain, if such your dealings.

MARCH 13

Julian – Oration 6

---

[19] A Cyrenaic philosopher considered to be an atheist

"For" says Diogenes, "it is not among men who
live on bread that you will find tyrants, but among
those who eat costly dinners."

MARCH 14

Diogenes Laertius – Book 6.34

Once, when some strangers wished to see
Demosthenes, [Diogenes] stretched out his middle
finger, and said, "This is the great demagogue of
the Athenian people."

MARCH 15

Greek Anthology 334 – On the Stone

Even brass is aged by time, but not all the ages,
Diogenes, shall destroy thy fame, since thou alone
didst show to mortals the rule of self-sufficiency
and the easiest path of life.

MARCH 16

Diogenes Laertius – Book 6.49

A man once reproached [Diogenes] with his
banishment, and his answer was, "You wretched
man, that is what made me a philosopher."

What makes you is not always planned. Often life
happens and we have to follow along on its
coattails.

MARCH 17

Aelian – Varia Historia 9.34 — Of Persons Richly
Clad

Diogenes coming to Olympia, and seeing the
seriousness some young Rhodian men, richly
attired, [Diogenes], laughing, said, "This is pride."
Then meeting with some Lacedemonians[20] clad in
coats coarse and sordid, "This (said he) is another
pride."

MARCH 18

Diogenes Laertius – Book 6.45

He saw a man giving himself airs because he was
clad in a lion's skin, and said to him, "Do not go
on disgracing the garb of nature."

MARCH 19

Diogenes Laertius – Book 6.46

On one occasion [Diogenes] was working with his
hands in the market-place, and said, "I wish I
could rub my stomach in the same way, and so
avoid hunger."

MARCH 20

---

[20] Lacedaemon is the region where Sparta is located

Diogenes Laertius – Book 6.44

On which account [Diogenes] said to a man, who had his shoes put on by his servant, "You are not thoroughly happy, unless he also wipes your nose for you; and he will do this, if you are crippled in your hands."

MARCH 21

Lucian – Demonax excerpts

For, though [Demonax] had leanings as regards externals and plain living to Diogenes, he never studied effect or lived for the applause and admiration of the multitude; his ways were like other people's; he mounted no high horse; he was just a man and a citizen.

MARCH 22

Diogenes Laertius – Book 6.52

Seeing some women hanging on olive trees, [Diogenes] said, "I wish every tree bore similar fruit."

MARCH 23

Diogenes Laertius – Book 6.29

The question was put to him what countryman he

was, and he replied, "A Citizen of the world"
(kosmopolites).

MARCH 24

Diogenes Laertius – Book 6.45

Once, too, some boys got round [Diogenes] and
said, "We are taking care that you do not bite us;"
but he said, "Be of good cheer, my boys, a dog
does not eat beef."

MARCH 25

Diogenes Laertius – Book 2.78

[Aristippus] used to complain of mankind that in
purchasing earthenware they made trial whether it
rang true, but had no regular standard by which to
judge life. Others attribute this remark to
Diogenes.

MARCH 26

Clement – Stromata 8.4

If you had propounded the question, Whether a
dog were an animal? For I might have rightly said,
Of what dog do you speak? For I shall speak of
the land dog and the sea dog, and the constellation
in heaven, and of Diogenes too, and all the other
dogs in order. For I could not divine whether you
inquire about all or about someone.

MARCH 27

Diogenes Laertius – Book 6.53

When Plato was discoursing about his "ideas,"
and using the nouns "tableness" and "cupness;"
"I, Plato!" interrupted Diogenes, "see a table and a
cup, but I see no tableness or cupness." Plato
made answer, "That is natural enough, for you
have eyes, by which a cup and a table are
contemplated; but you have not intellect, by which
tableness and cupness are seen."

MARCH 28

Plutarch – Of the Tranquillity of the Mind

That saying of Diogenes extremely pleases me,
who, seeing one sprucing himself up very neatly to
go to a great entertainment, asked him whether
every day was not a festival to a good man.

MARCH 29

Diogenes Laertius – Book 6.54

Another time, the question was put to [Diogenes],
when a man ought to marry? And his reply was,
"Young men ought not to marry yet, and old men
never ought to marry at all."

MARCH 30

Diogenes Laertius – Book 6.71

[Diogenes] used to say also, that there was nothing whatever in life which could be brought to perfection without practice, and that that alone was able to overcome every obstacle; that, therefore, as we ought to repudiate all useless toils, and to apply ourselves to useful labours and to live happily, we are only unhappy in consequence of most exceeding folly.

MARCH 31

Plutarch – The First Oration of Plutarch Concerning the Fortune of Virtue of Alexander the Great

Alexander was wont to say, Were I not Alexander, I would be Diogenes. That is, I would have devoted myself to the study of words, had I not been a philosopher in deeds. He did not say, Were I not a king, I would be Diogenes; nor, were I not opulent, an Argeades[21]. For he did not prefer fortune before wisdom, nor the purple robe or regal diadem before the beggar's wallet and threadbare mantle; but he said, were I not Alexander, I would be Diogenes.

---

[21] Member of the founding and ruling dynasty of the kingdom of Macedon

APRIL

APRIL 1

Cicero – Tusculan Disputations 1.43

Diogenes was rougher, though of the same
opinion; but in his character of a Cynic he
expressed himself in a somewhat harsher manner;
he ordered himself to be thrown anywhere
without being buried. And when his friends
replied, "What! to the birds and beasts?" "By no
means," said he; "place my staff near me, that I
may drive them away." "How can you do that,"
they answer, "for you will not perceive them?"
"How am I then injured by being torn by those
animals, if I have no sensation?"

APRIL 2

Diogenes Laertius – Book 6.72

[Diogenes] also argued about the law, that without
it there is no possibility of a constitution being
maintained; for without a city there can be
nothing orderly, but a city is an orderly thing; and
without a city there can be no law; therefore law is
order.

APRIL 3

Diogenes Laertius – Book 6.27

One of [Diogenes'] frequent sayings was, "That
men contended with one another in punching and

kicking, but that no one showed any emulation in
the pursuit of virtue."

APRIL 4

Diogenes Laertius – Book 6.52

At another time, [Diogenes] saw a clothes' stealer,
and addressed him thus: What moves you, say,
when sleep has closed the sight, to roam the silent
fields in dead of night?

APRIL 5

Diogenes Laertius – Book 6.33

On one occasion [Diogenes] went half shaved into
an entertainment of young men and so was beaten
by them. And afterwards he wrote the names of
all those who had beaten him on a white tablet,
and went about with the tablet round his neck, so
as to expose them to insult, as they were generally
condemned and reproached for their conduct.

APRIL 6

Diogenes Laertius – Book 6.69

[Diogenes] went once into a school, and saw many
statues of the Muses, but very few pupils, and said,
"Gods, and all my good schoolmasters, you have
plenty of pupils."

APRIL 7

Seneca – "On Benefits"

In benefits I must of necessity be outdone by
Socrates, of necessity by Diogenes, who marched
naked through the midst of the treasures of the
Macedonians, treading underfoot the wealth of
kings. O! In very truth, how rightly did he seem
then, both to himself and to all others who had
not been rendered blind to the perception of
truth, to tower above the man beneath whose feet
lay the whole world! Far more powerful, far richer
was he than Alexander, who then was master of
the whole world; for what Diogenes refused to
receive was even more than Alexander was able to
give.

APRIL 8

Aelian – Varia Historia 13.28 – Of the Servant of
Diogenes Torn in Pieces by Dogs

When Diogenes left his country, one of his
servants followed him; who not tolerating his
conversation ran away. Some persuading Diogenes
to make enquiry after him, he said, "Is it not a
shame that Manes should not need Diogenes, and
that Diogenes should need Manes?" But this
Servant wandering to Delphos, was torn in pieces
by Dogs, paying to his masters name [the Cynic,
aka Dog] the punishment of his running away.

APRIL 9

Aelian – Varia Historia 14.33 – Of Plato and
Diogenes.

Diogenes being present at a discourse of Plato's,
would not mind it, where Plato angry said, "Thou
Dog, why mindest thou not? Diogenes unmoved,
answered, "Yet I never return to the place where I
was sold, as Dogs do"; alluding to Plato's Voyage
to Sicily[22]. It is reported that Plato used to say of
Diogenes, "This man is Socrates mad."

APRIL 10

Plutarch – A Discourse Touching the Training of
Children 7

If now [children] had but conversed with some
philosopher, they would never have enslaved
themselves to such courses as these; though
possibly they might have learned at least to put in
practice the precept of Diogenes, delivered by him
indeed in rude language, but yet containing, as to
the scope of it, a great truth, when he advised a
young man to go to the public stews, that he
might then inform himself, by experience, how
things of greatest value and things of no value at
all were there of equal worth.

---

[22] Plato was invited to Sicily to educate Dionysius II, but ended up
returning to Athens after Dionysius II failed to take up philosophy.

APRIL 11

Diogenes Laertius – Book 6.63

Some men were sacrificing to the Gods to prevail
on them to send them sons, and he said, "And do
you not sacrifice to procure sons of a particular
character?"

APRIL 12

Apuleius – Florida 14

These arguments and the like which he had heard
from the lips of Diogenes, together with others
which suggested themselves to him on other
occasions, had such influence with Crates[23], that at
last he rushed out into the market-place and there
renounced all his fortune as being a mere filthy
encumbrance, a burden rather than a benefit.

APRIL 13

Diogenes Laertius – Book 6.39

After having anointed his feet with perfume,
[Diogenes] said that the ointment from his head
mounted up to heaven, and that from his feet up
to his nose.

---

[23] Cynic follower and successor to Diogenes

APRIL 14

Diogenes Laertius – Book 6.65

When a man said to him, "I am not calculated for philosophy," he said, "Why then do you live, if you have no desire to live properly?"

APRIL 15

Basil of Caesarea – Letter 9

But why, my dear sir, should you not pay me a visit, that we may talk of these high topics face to face, instead of committing them to lifeless letters—especially when I have determined not to publish my views? And pray do not adopt, to me, the words of Diogenes to Alexander, that "it is as far from you to me as from me to you." I am almost obliged by ill-health to remain like the plants, in one place; moreover I hold "the living unknown" to be one of the chief goods.

APRIL 16

Diogenes Laertius – Book 6.46

Once at a banquet, some of the guests threw him bones, as if [Diogenes] had been a dog; so he, as he went away, put up his leg against them as if he had been a dog in reality.

APRIL 17

Diogenes Laertius – Book 6.56

When some one reproached him for having tampered with the coinage[24], he said, "There was a time when I was such a person as you are now; but there never was when you were such as I am now, and never will be."

APRIL 18

Diogenes Laertius – Book 6.59

A certain person was admiring the offerings in the temple at Samothrace[25], and he said to him, "They would have been much more numerous, if those who were lost had offered them instead of those who were saved."

APRIL 19

Diogenes Laertius – Book 6.25

On one occasion, when he noticed Plato at a very costly entertainment tasting some olives, he said, "O you wise man! why, after having sailed to Sicily for the sake of such a feast, do you not now enjoy what you have before you?" And Plato replied,

---

[24] Diogenes was exiled from his native Sinope, a Greek city on the Black Sea, due to defacing the currency of the city.
[25] The cult at Samothrace was popular with mariners and fishermen

"By the Gods, Diogenes, while I was there I ate
olives and all such things a great deal." Diogenes
rejoined, "What then did you want to sail to
Syracuse for? Did not Attica[26] at that time produce
any olives?" But this story is told of Aristippus.

APRIL 20

Diogenes Laertius – Book 6.66

He once said to a man who was addressing
anxious entreaties to a courtesan, "What can you
wish to obtain, you wretched man, that you had
not better be disappointed in?

APRIL 21

Diogenes Laertius – Book 6.28

"That misers blamed money, but were
preposterously fond of it." He often condemned
those who praise the just for being superior to
money, but who at the same time are eager
themselves for great riches.

APRIL 22

Diogenes Laertius – Book 6.57

When Craterus[27] entreated him to come and visit

---

[26] Attica is the region of Greece where Athens is located

him, he said, "I would rather lick up salt at
Athens, than enjoy a luxurious table with
Craterus."

APRIL 23

Pausanias – Description of Greece 2.2.4

As one goes up to Corinth are tombs, and by the
gate is buried Diogenes of Sinope, whom the
Greeks surname the Dog.

APRIL 24

Julian – Oration 6

Yet this even the wise Socrates thought he did not
know, yes and after him Diogenes as well.

APRIL 25

Aulus Gellius – Attic Nights 1.2

"Of all existing things some are good, some evil,
and some indifferent. Now the good things are
virtues and what partakes of them, the evil are vice
and what partakes of vice, and the indifferent lie
between these: wealth, health, life, death, pleasure,
pain. "How do you know this?" For what
difference does it make whether you say that, or

---

[27] Macedonian general and a successor to Alexander the Great

that it was Diogenes in his *Ethics* or Chrysippus or
Cleanthes[28]?

APRIL 26

Aelian – Varia Historia 8.14 – Of the Death of
Diogenes

Diogenes the Sinopean, being sick to death, and
scarce able to go, cast himself from a bridge which
was near the place of exercise, and charged the
keeper of the place that as soon as he was quite
dead, he should throw him into the [River] Ilissus[29];
so little did Diogenes value death or burial.

APRIL 27

Julian – Oration 6

For Diogenes preferred to live in Athens, but
when the divine command had sent him away to
Corinth, even after he had been set free by the
man who had bought him, he did not think he
ought to leave that city. For he believed that the
gods took care of him, and that he had been sent
to Corinth, not at random or by some accident,
but by the gods themselves for some purpose. He
saw that Corinth was more luxurious than Athens,
and stood in need of a more severe and
courageous reformer.

---

[28] Stoic philosophers
[29] River that ran outside the defensive border wall of Athens

APRIL 28

Diogenes Laertius – Book 6.68

When Didymus the adulterer was once trying to cure the eye of a young girl (kore), he said, "Take care, lest when you are curing the eye of the maiden, you do not hurt the pupil (kore)."

APRIL 29

Dio Chrysostom – The Sixth Discourse – Diogenes, or On Tyranny

"Still, all human ills admit of this one consolation," continued Diogenes — "they may possibly come to an end. The prisoner in chains expects some time to be set free; it is not impossible for the exile to return to his home; and he who is sick can hope until the end comes for recovery. But the tyrant may not escape his condition; no, he cannot even so much as pray except it be for something else. Anyone who has suffered the loss of a friend by death believes in his heart that time will eventually heal his grief; but tyrants, on the contrary, find their troubles growing worse and worse; since it is not easy for a tyrant to reach old age, and a tyrant's old age is grievous."

APRIL 30

Tertullian – Ad Nationes 2.2

Diogenes, when asked what was taking place in
heaven, answered by saying, "I have never been
up there." Again, whether there were any gods, he
replied, "I do not know; only there ought to be
gods."

MAY

MAY 1

Julian – Oration 6

For the much-talked-of tragedies of Diogenes are
now said to be the work of a certain Philiscus of
Aegina[30]; though even if they were by Diogenes
there would be nothing out of the way in a wise
man's jesting, since many philosophers have been
known to do so.

MAY 2

Diogenes Laertius – Book 6.49

Once [Diogenes] was begging of someone (for he
did this at first out of actual want), he said, "If you
have given to anyone else, give also to me; and if
you have never given to anyone, then begin with
me."

MAY 3

Diogenes Laertius – Book 6.40

Some mice crept up to his table, and he said, "see,
even Diogenes maintains his favourites."

MAY 4

---

[30] Cynic Philosopher from the city of Aegina who became charmed
with Diogenes' way of life

Diogenes Laertius – Book 6.59

Once [Diogenes] saw a handsome youth going to
a banquet, and said to him, "You will come back
worse (cheirôn);" and when he the next day after
the banquet said to him, "I have left the banquet,
and was no worse for it;" he replied, "You were
not Chiron, but Eurytion[31]."

MAY 5

Aelian – Varia Historia 12.56 — What Diogenes
said of the Megareans

Diogenes the Sinopean said many things to
censure the ignorance and lack of discipline of the
Megareans[32], and would rather choose to be a ram
belonging to a Megarean, then his son. He implied
that the Megareans had great care of their flocks,
but none of their children.

MAY 6

Diogenes Laertius – Book 6.21

When [Diogenes] came to Athens he attached
himself to Antisthenes[33]; but as he repelled him,

---

[31] Chiron was the mythical centaur teacher of many Greek heroes and
demi-gods. Eurytion was a wild, violent centaur, who in most
traditions is killed by Heracles
[32] People living in the Greek town of Megara located in West Attica,
which is the same region as Athens.
[33] Teacher of Diogenes and considered the first Cynic. Antisthenes

because he admitted no one; he at last forced his way to him by his pertinacity. And once, when he raised his stick at him, he put his head under it, and said, "strike, for you will not find any stick hard enough to drive me away as long as you continue to speak." And from this time forth he was one of his pupils; and being an exile, he naturally betook himself to a simple mode of life.

MAY 7

Diogenes Laertius – Book 6.61

On one occasion [Diogenes] was eating his dinner in the marketplace, and the bystanders kept constantly calling out "Dog;" but he said, "It is you who are the dogs, who stand around me while I am at dinner."

MAY 8

Diogenes Laertius – Book 6.41

[Diogenes] used to say that the demagogues were the servants of the people; and garlands the blossoms of glory. Having lighted a candle in the day time, he said, "I am looking for a man."

MAY 9

---

was a direct follower of Socrates.

Diogenes Laertius – Book 6.37

On one occasion [Diogenes] saw a child drinking
out of its hands, and so he threw away the cup
which belonged to his wallet, saying, "That child
has beaten me in simplicity." He also threw away
his spoon, after seeing a boy, when he had broken
his vessel, take up his lentils with a crust of bread.

MAY 10

Diogenes Laertius – Book 6.36

Once a man came to [Diogenes], and wished to
study philosophy as his pupil; and he gave him a
saperda[34] and made him follow him. And as he
from shame threw it away and departed, he soon
afterwards met him and, laughing, said to him, "A
saperda has dissolved your friendship for me."

MAY 11

Diogenes Laertius – Book 6.54

Having once listened to two lawyers, [Diogenes]
condemned them both; saying, "That the one had
stolen the thing in question, and that the other
had not lost it."

MAY 12

---

[34] A salted fish of little value

Diogenes Laertius – Book 6.47

[Diogenes] said that a rich but ignorant man, was
like a sheep with a golden fleece.

MAY 13

Diogenes Laertius – Book 6.60

Another time [Diogenes] was returning from the
Olympic games, and when someone asked him
whether there had been a great multitude there, he
said, "A great multitude, but very few men."

MAY 14

Julian – Oration 6

For "Know Thyself" he addressed not only to
Diogenes, but to other men also and still does: for
it stands there engraved in front of his shrine. And
so we have at last discovered the founder of this
philosophy, we have discovered its leading men as
well, namely Antisthenes and Diogenes and
Crates; the aim and end of whose lives was, I
think, to know themselves, to despise vain
opinions, and to lay hold of truth with their whole
understanding; for truth, alike for gods and men,
is the beginning of every good thing;.

MAY 15

Plutarch – How a Man May Receive Advantage
and Profit from his Enemies

There are others who, as Diogenes and Crates did,
have made banishment from their native country
and loss of all their goods a means to pass out of a
troublesome world into the quiet and serene state
of philosophy and mental contemplation.

MAY 16

Diogenes Laertius – Book 6.64

[Diogenes] used to say, that those who utter
virtuous sentiments but do not do them, are no
better than harps, for that a harp has no hearing
or feeling.

MAY 17

Aelian – Varia Historia 9.19 — That
Demosthenes refused, being called by Diogenes to
go into a Cook's Shop

As on a time Diogenes was at dinner in a cook's
shop, he called to Demosthenes[35] who passed by.
But he taking no notice, "Do you think it a
disparagement, Demosthenes, (said he) to come
into a cook's shop? Your Master comes hither

---

[35] Greek statesman and orator of ancient Athens. Significant public
figure in his time, mostly known for his protestations against Ancient
Macedon and Philip.

every day"; meaning the common people, and
implying that orators and lawyers are servants of
the vulgar.

MAY 18

Lucian – Dialogues of the Dead excerpts

Diogenes [said]: But, my handsome Mausolus[36],
the power and the beauty are no longer there. If
we were to appoint an umpire now on the
question of comeliness, I see no reason why he
should prefer your skull to mine. Both are bald,
and bare of flesh; our teeth are equally in
evidence; each of us has lost his eyes, and each is
snub-nosed. Then as to the tomb and the costly
marbles, I dare say such a fine erection gives the
Halicarnassians something to brag about and
show off to strangers: but I don"t see, friend, that
you are the better for it, unless it is that you claim
to carry more weight than the rest of us, with all
that marble on the top of you.

MAY 19

Diogenes Laertius – Book 6.66

Seeing a man reeking all over with ointments,
[Diogenes] said to him, "Have a care, lest the

---

[36] Mausolos is best known for the monumental shrine, the
Mausoleum at Halicarnassus.

fragrance of your head give a bad odour to your
life."

Diogenes Laertius – Book 6.28

[Diogenes] was also very indignant at seeing men
sacrifice to the Gods to procure good health, and
yet at the sacrifice eating in a manner injurious to
health. He often expressed his surprise at slaves,
who, seeing their masters eating in a gluttonous
manner, still do not themselves lay hands on any
of the eatables.

Clement of Alexandria – Pedagogy 3.3

Diogenes, when he was being sold, chiding like a
teacher one of these degenerate creatures, said
very manfully, Come, youngster, buy for yourself a
man, chastising his meretriciousness by an
ambiguous speech.

Diogenes Laertius – Book 6.40

Plato defined man thus: "Man is a two-footed,
featherless animal;" and was much praised for the
definition; so Diogenes plucked a cock and
brought it into his school, and said, "This is

Plato's man." On which account this addition was
made to the definition, "With broad flat nails."

MAY 24

Diogenes Laertius – Book 6.28

[Diogenes] used to express his astonishment at the
grammarians for being desirous to learn
everything about the misfortunes of Odysseus,
and being ignorant of their own. He used also to
say, "That the musicians fitted the strings to the
lyre properly, but left all the habits of their soul ill-
arranged." And, "That mathematicians kept their
eyes fixed on the sun and moon, and overlooked
what was under their feet." "That orators were
anxious to speak justly, but not at all about acting
so."

MAY 25

Julian – Oration 6

Then let him who wishes to be a Cynic, earnest
and sincere, first take himself in hand like
Diogenes and Crates, and expel from his own soul
and from every part of it all passions and desires,
and entrust all his affairs to reason and intelligence
and steer his course by them. For this in my
opinion was the sum and substance of the
philosophy of Diogenes.

MAY 26

Diogenes Laertius – Book 4.3

At last in old age [Diogenes] became so despondent that he put an end to his life. Here follows my epigram upon him: Had I not learnt that Speusippus[37] would die thus, no one would have persuaded me to say that he was surely not of Plato's blood; for else he would never have died in despair for a trivial cause.

MAY 27

Diogenes Laertius – Book 6.29

Menippus[38], in his *Sale of Diogenes*, says that he was taken prisoner and put up to be sold, and asked what he could do; and he answered, "Govern men."

MAY 28

Diogenes Laertius – Book 6.55

When a man said to him, that it was a bad thing to live; "Not to live," said [Diogenes], "but to live badly."

---

[37] An ancient Greek philosopher and successor of Plato. Speusippus was Plato's nephew by his sister Potone.
[38] Cynic Philosopher well known for his satirical treatise. The type of satire known as "Menippean Satire" is named after him.

MAY 29

Plutarch – How to Know a Flatterer from a
Friend 30

As pert was that of Diogenes, who, entering
Philip's camp as he was going to make war upon
the Grecians, was seized upon and brought before
the king, who not knowing him asked him if he
was a spy. Why, yes truly, said he, I am a spy upon
your folly and imprudence, who without any
necessity upon you are come hither to expose
your kingdoms and your life to the uncertain
decision of the cast of a die. This may perhaps
seem a little too biting and satirical.

MAY 30

Demetrius – On Style 260

So with a saying of Diogenes at Olympia[39], when
(at the conclusion of the race between the men in
armour) he ran up and proceeded to proclaim
himself victor at the Olympic games over all
mankind — in high personal character. This
exclamation excites mingled laughter and
applause, and there is a light touch of mordant wit
about it too.

---

[39] Small town in Elis on the Peloponnese peninsula in Greece,
famous for the nearby archaeological site of the same name, which
was a major Panhellenic religious sanctuary of ancient Greece, where
the ancient Olympic Games were held.

Plutarch – Whether an Aged Man Ought to
Meddle in State Affairs 1

For tyranny is not an honorable sepulchre, as one
told Dionysius, whose monarchy, obtained by and
administered with injustice, did by its long
continuance bring on him but a more perfect
calamity; as Diogenes afterwards let his son know,
when, seeing him at Corinth, of a tyrant become a
private person, he said to him: "How unworthy of
thyself, Dionysius, thou actest! For thou oughtest
not to live here at liberty and fearless with us, but
to spend thy life, as thy father did, even to old age,
immured within a tyrannical fortress.

JUNE

JUNE 1

Julian – Oration 6

Not that Diogenes tried to rival the gods, but he
lived more happily than one who is counted the
happiest of men, and he used actually to assert
that he lived more happily than such a man. And
if you do not believe me, try his mode of life in
deed and not in word, and you will perceive the
truth.

JUNE 2

Diogenes Laertius – Book 6.69

And as [Diogenes] was continually [masturbating]
in public, he said one day, "Would that by rubbing
my belly I could get rid of hunger." Other sayings
also are attributed to him, which it would take a
long time to enumerate, there is such a multiplicity
of them.

JUNE 3

Diogenes Laertius – Book 4.3

When [Diogenes] was already crippled by
paralysis, he sent a message to Xenocrates[40]
entreating him to come and take over the charge

---

[40] Platonist philosopher and leader of the Academy.

of the school. They say that, as he was being
conveyed to the Academy in a tiny carriage, he
met and saluted Diogenes, who replied, "Nay, if
you can endure to live in such a plight as this, I
decline to return your greeting."

JUNE 4

Diogenes Laertius – Book 6.41

When [Diogenes] was at Megara he saw some
sheep carefully covered over with skins, and the
children running about naked; and so he said, "It
is better at Megara to be a man's ram, than his
son."

JUNE 5

Aelian – Varia Historia 10.11 — Of Diogenes
having a Pain in his Shoulder

Diogenes had a pain in his Shoulder by some hurt,
as I conceive, or from some other cause: and
seeming to be much troubled, one that was
present being vexed at him, derided him, saying,
"Why then do you not die, Diogenes, and free
your self from ills?" He answered, "It was fit those
persons who knew what was to be done and said
in life, (of which he professed himself one) should
live. Wherefore for you (saith he) who know
neither what is fit to be said or done, it is
convenient to die; but me, who know these things,
it behoveth to live."

JUNE 6

Diogenes Laertius – Book 6.45

When people were speaking of the happiness of
Callisthenes[41], and saying what splendid treatment
he received from Alexander, [Diogenes] replied,
"The man then is wretched, for he is forced to
breakfast and dine whenever Alexander chooses."

JUNE 7

Diogenes Laertius – Book 6.55

When some people were advising [Diogenes] to
make search for a slave who had run away,"
[Diogenes] said, "It would be a very absurd thing
for Manes to be able to live without Diogenes, but
for Diogenes not to be able to live without
Manes."

JUNE 8

Diogenes Laertius – Book 6.35

Another of [Diogenes'] sayings, was that most
men were within a finger's breadth of being mad.
If, then, any one were to walk along, stretching
out his middle finger, he will seem to be mad; but

---

[41] Well-connected Greek historian in Macedon who accompanied
Alexander the Great during the Asiatic expedition.

if he puts out his fore finger, he will not be
thought so.

JUNE 9

Diogenes Laertius – Book 6.58

When a man said to him once, "Most people
laugh at you;" "And very likely," [Diogenes]
replied, "the asses laugh at them; but they do not
regard the asses, neither do I regard them."

JUNE 10

Diogenes Laertius – Book 6.49

When he was asked why athletes are insensible to
pain, he said, "Because they are built up of pork
and beef."

JUNE 11

Diogenes Laertius – Book 6.64

When all the company was blaming an indifferent
harp-player, [Diogenes] alone praised him and
being asked why he did so, he said, "Because,
though he is such as he is, he plays the harp and
does not steal." He saluted a harp player who was
always left alone by his hearers, with, "Good
morning, cock;" and when the man asked him,
"Why so?" he said, "Because you, when you sing,
make everyone get up."

JUNE 12

Diogenes Laertius – Book 6.51

One of [Diogenes'] apophthegms was, that good
men were the images of the Gods; another, that
love was the business of those who had nothing to
do.

JUNE 13

Diogenes Laertius – Book 6.24

[Diogenes] said that the *schole* (school) of Euclides
was *chole* (gall).

JUNE 14

Diogenes Laertius – Book 6.25

At another time [Diogenes] was eating dried figs,
when Plato met him, and he said to him, "You
may have a share of these;" and as he took some
and ate them, he said, "I said that you might have
a share of them, not that you might eat them all."

JUNE 15

Diogenes Laertius – Book 6.35

[Diogenes] used to say, that he imitated the
teachers of choruses, for that they spoke too loud
in order that the rest might catch the proper tone.

JUNE 16

Plutarch – How to Know a Flatterer from a
Friend 36

As Diogenes said pertinently enough to this
purpose, that he who would act wisely ought to be
surrounded either with good friends or flagrant
enemies; for the one always teach us well, and the
other as constantly accuse us if we do ill.

JUNE 17

Diogenes Laertius – Book 6.56

The question was put to [Diogenes], whether wise
men ate cheese-cakes, and he replied, "They eat
everything, just as the rest of mankind."

JUNE 18

Epictetus – Discourses 4.1

Therefore we will call only those creatures free,
that do not endure captivity, but escape by death
as soon as they are caught. So too Diogenes says
somewhere, "A quiet death is the one sure means
of freedom", and he writes to the Persian king,
"You cannot enslave the city of the Athenians any
more than you can enslave fishes."

JUNE 19

Aelian – Varia Historia 10.16 — Of Antisthenes
and Diogenes

Antisthenes invited many to learn Philosophy of
him, but none came. At last, growing angry, he
would admit none at all, and therefore bade
Diogenes be gone also. Diogenes continuing to
come frequently, he chide and threatened him,
and at last struck him with his Staff. Diogenes
would not go back, but persisting still in desire of
hearing him, said, "strike if you will, here is my
head, you cannot find a Staff hard enough to drive
me from you, until you have instructed me."
Antisthenes overcome with his perseverance,
admitted him, and made him his intimate Friend.

JUNE 20

Jerome – Against Jovinian 2.14

[Antisthenes] most famous follower was the great
Diogenes, who was mightier than King Alexander
in that he conquered human nature. For
Antisthenes would not take a single pupil, and
when he could not get rid of the persistent
Diogenes he threatened him with a stick if he did
not depart. The latter is said to have laid down his
head and said, No stick will be hard enough to
prevent me from following you.

JUNE 21

Diogenes Laertius – Book 6.62

Being once asked about a debauched boy, as to
what country he came from, [Diogenes] said, "He
is a Tegean."[42]

JUNE 22

Diogenes Laertius – Book 6.64

When supping in a temple, as some dirty loaves
were set before him, [Diogenes] took them up and
threw them away, saying that nothing dirty ought
to come into a temple; and when someone said to
him, "You philosophize without being possessed
of any knowledge," he said, "If I only pretend to
wisdom, that is philosophizing."

JUNE 23

Diogenes Laertius – Book 6.34

Once [Diogenes] attempted to eat raw meat, but
he could not digest it.

JUNE 24

Aristotle – Rhetoric 1411a24

---

[42] This is a pun on the similarity of sound of Tegea to tegos, a
brothel.

[Diogenes] the Cynic used to say that the taverns were "the messes" of Attica.

JUNE 25

Diogenes Laertius – Book 6.32

They also relate that Alexander said that if he had not been Alexander, he should have liked to be Diogenes.

JUNE 26

Tertullian – Apology Chapter 46

If I maintain our superior modesty of behaviour, there at once occurs to me Diogenes with filth-covered feet trampling on the proud couches of Plato, under the influence of another pride: the Christian does not even play the proud man to the pauper.

JUNE 27

Diogenes Laertius – Book 6.49

And when, on another occasion, someone said to [Diogenes], "The people of Sinope condemned you to banishment," he replied, "And I condemned them to remain where they were."

JUNE 28

Diogenes Laertius – Book 6.105

Some at all events are vegetarians and drink cold water only and are content with any kind of shelter or tubs, like Diogenes, who used to say that it was the privilege of the gods to need nothing and of god-like men to want but little.

JUNE 29

Dio Chrysostom – The Sixth Discourse – Diogenes, or On Tyranny

When Diogenes of Sinope was exiled from that place, he came to Greece and used to divide his time between Corinth and Athens. And he said he was following the practice of the Persian king. For that monarch spent the winters in Babylon and Susa, or occasionally in Bactra, which are the warmest parts of Asia, and the summers in Median Ecbatana, where the air is always very cool and the summer is like the winter in the region of Babylon[43].

JUNE 30

Diogenes Laertius – Book 6.62

---

[43] The Persian king moved seasonally to different capitals throughout the vast Persian Empire. Babylon, Susa, and Bactra were chosen for winter residence since they were warm, and Ecbatana was chosen for it's cool temperature in the summer.

He was asked by someone to give him back his
cloak; but [Diogenes] replied, "If you gave it me, it
is mine; and if you only lent it me, I am using it."

JULY

JULY 1

Epictetus – Discourses 2.3

That is a good answer of Diogenes to one who
asked him for letters of introduction: "You are a
man, and that his eyes will tell him; but whether
you are good or bad he will discover, if he has skill
to distinguish the good from the bad; and if he has
not that skill, he will never discover it, though I
should write him ten thousand letters."

JULY 2

Plutarch – Lives of the Ten Orators,
"Demosthenes"

Diogenes the Cynic espying him one day in a
victualling-house, he was very much ashamed, and
to shun him, went to withdraw; but Diogenes
called after him, and told him, The more you
shrink inward, the more you will be in the tavern.
The same Diogenes once upon the banter said of
him, that in his orations he was a Scythian[44], but in
war a delicate nice citizen.

JULY 3

Diogenes Laertius – Book 6.18

---

[44] Nomadic people who are often used as examples of barbarity.

He died of disease just as Diogenes, who had
come in, inquired of him, "Have you need of a
friend?" Once too Diogenes, when he came to
him, brought a dagger. And when Antisthenes
cried out, "Who will release me from these
pains?" replied, "This," showing him the dagger.
"I said," quoth the other, "from my pains, not
from life."

JULY 4

Diogenes Laertius – Book 6.56

And to another person who reproached
[Diogenes] on the same grounds, he said, "There
were times when I did what I did not wish to, but
that is not the case now."

JULY 5

Diogenes Laertius – Book 6.35

Another of [Diogenes'] sayings was, that things of
great value were often sold for nothing, and vice
versa. Accordingly, that a statue would fetch three
thousand drachmas, and a bushel of meal only
two obols; and when Xeniades had bought him,
he said to him, "Come, do what you are ordered
to." And when he said - "The streams of sacred
rivers now, run backwards to their source!"

JULY 6

Diogenes Laertius – Book 6.67

Being asked why slaves were called andrapoda, [Diogenes] replied, "Because they have the feet of men (*tous podas andron*) and a soul such as you who are asking this question."

JULY 7

Diogenes Laertius – Book 6.61

On one occasion [Diogenes] was gathering some of the fruit of a fig-tree, and when the man who was guarding it told him a man hung himself on this tree the other day, "I, then," said he, "will now purify it."

JULY 8

Lucian – Dialogues of the Dead excerpts

Alexander. I have lain in Babylon a full month today; and Ptolemy of the Guards[45] is pledged, as soon as he can get a moment's respite from present disturbances, to take and bury me in Egypt, there to be reckoned among the Gods.

Diogenes. There is one thing I wish you would tell me: how do you like thinking over all the earthly bliss you left to come here — your guards and

---

[45] The Ptolemies in Ancient Egypt held an elite force to guard

armour-bearers and lieutenant-governors, your heaps of gold and adoring peoples, Babylon and Bactria, your huge elephants, your honour and glory, those conspicuous drives with white-cinctured locks and clasped purple cloak? does the thought of them hurt ? What, crying? silly fellow! did not your wise Aristotle include in his instructions any hint of the insecurity of fortune's favours?

JULY 9

Diogenes Laertius – Book 6.51

When the question was put to him, why gold is of a pale colour, [Diogenes] said, "Because it has so many people plotting against it."

JULY 10

Antiphilus of Byzantium –Greek Anthology 333 – On Diogenes

The wallet and cloak and the barley-dough thickened with water, the staff planted before his feet, and the earthenware cup, are estimated by the wise Dog as sufficient for the needs of life, and even in these there was something superfluous; for, seeing the countryman drinking from the hollow of his hand, he said, "Why, thou earthen cup, did I burden myself with thee to no purpose".

JULY 11

Diogenes Laertius – Book 2.68

Diogenes, washing the dirt from his vegetables, saw [Plato] passing and jeered at him in these terms, "If you had learnt to make these your diet, you would not have paid court to kings," to which his rejoinder was, "And if you knew how to associate with men, you would not be washing vegetables."

JULY 12

Diogenes Laertius – Book 6.24

It was also a saying of [Diogenes'] that the Dionysian games were a great marvel to fools; and that the demagogues were the ministers of the multitude.

JULY 13

Diogenes Laertius – Book 6.44

Once, when Alexander had sent a letter to Athens to Antipater[46], by the hands of a man named Athlias, [Diogenes], being present, said, "Athlias from Athlius, by means of Athlias to Athlius" or

---

[46] Macedonian general and statesman under kings Philip II of Macedon and Alexander the Great

"Graceless son of graceless sire to graceless spirit
by graceless squire"

JULY 14

Juvenal, Satire 14

Wealth gotten with such woes is preserved by
fears and troubles that are greater still; it is misery
to have the guardianship of a great fortune. The
millionaire Licinus orders a troop of slaves to be
on the watch all night with fire buckets in their
places, being anxious for his amber, his statues
and Phrygian marbles, his ivory and plaques of
tortoise-shell. The nude Cynic [Diogenes] fears no
fire for his tub; if broken, he will make himself a
new house tomorrow, or repair it with clamps of
lead. When Alexander beheld in that tub its
mighty occupant, he felt how much happier was
the man who had no desires than he who claimed
for himself the entire world, with perils before
him as great as his achievements. Had we but
wisdom, thou wouldst have no Divinity, O
Fortune: it is we that make thee into a Goddess!

JULY 15

Diogenes Laertius – Book 6.22

In reference to which habit [Diogenes] used to
say, pointing to the Colonnade of [Zeus], and to
the Public Magazine [i.e. Hall of Processions][47],

"that the Athenians had built him places to live in."

JULY 16

Lucian – Dialogues of the Dead excerpts

But here we are at the gate; we must keep our eyes open, and get the earliest view. Lord, lord, what a mixed crowd! and all in tears except these babes and sucklings. Why, the hoary seniors are all lamentation too; strange! has madam Life given them a love-potion? I must interrogate this most reverend senior of them all. - Sir, why weep, seeing that you have died full of years? has your excellency any complaint to make, after so long a term? Ah, but you were doubtless a king.

JULY 17

Diogenes Laertius – Book 6.68

When [Diogenes] was asked whether death was an evil, he replied, "How can that be an evil which we do not feel when it is present?"

JULY 18

---

[47] The Colonnade of Zeus and Public Magazine were public gathering places in Athens.

Julian – Oration 6

For it is evident that Diogenes was not impious, as
you aver, but resembled those philosophers whom
I mentioned a moment ago. For having regard to
the circumstances in which his lot was cast, and
next paying heed to the commands of the Pythian[48]
god, and knowing that the candidate for initiation
must first be registered as an Athenian citizen, and
if he be not an Athenian by birth must first
become one by law, it was this he avoided, not
initiation, because he considered that he was a
citizen of the world; and moreover such was the
greatness of his soul that he thought he ought to
associate himself with the divine nature of all the
gods who in common govern the whole universe,
and not only with those whose functions are
limited to certain portions of it.

JULY 19

Diogenes Laertius – Book 6.40

Once, when [Diogenes] was leaving the bath, and
a man asked him whether many men were
bathing, he said, "No;" but when a number of
people came out, he confessed that there were a
great many.

---

[48] Name of the high priestess of the Temple of Apollo at Delphi who
also served as the oracle, also known as the Oracle of Delphi.

JULY 20

Lucian – Dialogues of the Dead excerpts

Diogenes. Cleverly done. Now, when we were alive, we never had such designs on one another. I never prayed for Antisthenes's death, with a view to inheriting his staff — though it was an extremely serviceable one, which he had cut himself from a wild olive; and I do not credit you, Crates, with ever having had an eye to my succession; it included the tub, and a wallet with two pints of lupines in it.

JULY 21

Diogenes Laertius – Book 6.50

[Diogenes] used to say that greediness was the metropolis of all evils.

JULY 22

Augustine, City of God Book 14.20

It is this which those canine or cynic philosophers have overlooked, when they have, in violation of the modest instincts of men, boastfully proclaimed their unclean and shameless opinion, worthy indeed of dogs, viz., that as the matrimonial act is legitimate, no one should be ashamed to perform it openly, in the street or in any public place. Instinctive shame has overborne this wild fancy.

For though it is related that Diogenes once dared
to put his opinion in practice, under the
impression that his sect would be all the more
famous if his egregious shamelessness were deeply
graven in the memory of mankind, yet this
example was not afterwards followed. Shame had
more influence with them, to make them blush
before men, than error to make them affect a
resemblance to dogs. And possibly, even in the
case of Diogenes, and those who did imitate him,
there was but an appearance and pretence of
copulation, and not the reality. Even at this day
there are still Cynic philosophers to be seen; for
these are Cynics who are not content with being
clad in the pallium, but also carry a club; yet no
one of them dares to do this that we speak of. If
they did, they would be spat upon, not to say
stoned, by the mob. Human nature, then, is
without doubt ashamed of this lust; and justly so,
for the insubordination of these members, and
their defiance of the will, are the clear testimony
of the punishment of man's first sin. And it was
fitting that this should appear specially in those
parts by which is generated that nature which has
been altered for the worse by that first and great
sin — that sin from whose evil connection no one
can escape, unless God's grace expiate in him
individually that which was perpetrated to the
destruction of all in common, when all were in
one man, and which was avenged by God's
justice.

JULY 23

Plutarch – Of the Tranquillity of the Mind

Diogenes was driven into banishment, but it was "not so bad" for him; for of an exile he became a philosopher.

JULY 24

Diogenes Laertius – Book 6.46

And when some people were praising a man who had given him alms, [Diogenes] said to then, "And do not you praise me who was worthy to receive it?"

JULY 25

Diogenes Laertius – Book 6.49

[Diogenes] once asked for a statue; and being questioned as to his reason for doing so, he said, "I am practising disappointment."

JULY 26

Diogenes Laertius – Book 6.26

Diogenes once asked him for some wine, and then for some dried figs; so he sent him an entire jar full; and Diogenes said to him, "Will you, if you are asked how many two and two make, answer twenty? In this way, you neither give with any reference to what you are asked for, nor do you answer with reference to the question put to you." He used also to ridicule him as an interminable talker.

JULY 27

Jerome – Against Jovinian 2.14

[Diogenes'] virtue and self-restraint were proved even by his death. It is said that, now an old man, he was on his way to the Olympic games, which used to be attended by a great concourse of people from all parts of Greece, when he was overtaken by fever and lay down upon the bank by the road-side. And when his friends wished to place him on a beast or in a conveyance, he did not assent, but crossing to the shade of a tree said, Go your way, I pray you, and see the games: this night will prove me either conquered or conqueror. If I conquer the fever, I shall go to the games: if the fever conquers me, I shall enter the unseen world. There through the night he lay gasping for breath and did not, as we are told, so much die as banish the fever by death.

JULY 28

Diogenes Laertius – Book 6.37

Once [Diogenes] saw a woman falling down before the Gods in an unbecoming attitude; he, wishing to cure her of her superstition, came up to her, and said, "Are you not afraid, O woman, to be in such an indecent attitude, when some God may be behind you, for every place is full of him?"

JULY 29

Athenaeus – Deipnosophistae Book 8

Diogenes the Cynic also died when his belly swelled up after he had eaten a raw polyp.

JULY 30

Diogenes Laertius – Book 6.53

Seeing a handsome youth sleeping without any protection, [Diogenes] nudged him, and said, "Wake up: mixed with the vulgar shall thy fate be found, pierced in the back, a vile dishonest wound."

JULY 31

Julian – Oration 6

Behold the rivers are flowing backwards, as the proverb says! Here is a Cynic who says that Diogenes was conceited, and who refuses to take cold baths for fear they may injure him, though he has a very strong constitution and is lusty and in the prime of life, and this too though the Sun-god is now nearing the summer solstice.

AUGUST

AUGUST 1

Julian – Oration 6

Nay it is enough merely to hearken to the Pythian god when he enjoins these two precepts, "Know Thyself," and "Falsify the common currency." Hence it becomes evident to us that the founder of this philosophy is he who, I believe, is the cause of all the blessings that the Greeks enjoy, the universal leader, law-giver and king of Hellas, I mean the god of Delphi. And since it was not permitted that he should be in ignorance of everything, the peculiar fitness of Diogenes did not escape his notice. And he made him incline to that philosophy, not by urging his commands in words alone, as he does for other men, but in very deed he instructed him symbolically as to what he willed, in two words, when he said, "Falsify the common currency."

AUGUST 2

Diogenes Laertius – Book 6.40

A man once asked [Diogenes] what was the proper time for supper, and he made answer, "If you are a rich man, whenever you please; and if you are a poor man, whenever you can."

AUGUST 3

Diogenes Laertius – Book 6.30

[Diogenes] used to say, that he wondered at men always ringing a dish or jar before buying it, but being content to judge of a man by his look alone.

AUGUST 4

Diogenes Laertius – Book 6.50

Seeing on one occasion a [spendthrift] man in an inn eating olives, [Diogenes] said, "If you had dined thus, you would not have supped thus."

AUGUST 5

Philo – Every Good Man is Free 121-126

Accordingly the Cynic philosopher, Diogenes, exhibited such a loftiness and greatness of spirit, that when he was taken prisoner by some robbers, and when they fed him very sparingly, and scarcely gave him even necessary food, he was not weighed down by the circumstances which surrounded him, and did not fear the inhumanity of the masters into whose power he had fallen, but said "that it was a most absurd thing for pigs or sheep, when they were going to be sold, to be carefully provided with abundant food, so as to be rendered fat and fleshy; but for the most excellent of all animals, man, to be reduced to a skeleton by bad food and continual scarcity, and so to be rendered of less value than before."

Dio Chrysostom – The Ninth Discourse – The
Isthmian Discourse

On this occasion he saw two horses that were
hitched together fall to fighting and kicking each
other, with a large crowd standing by and looking
on, until one of the animals, becoming exhausted,
broke loose and ran off. Then Diogenes came up
and placed a crown upon the head of the horse
that had stood its ground and proclaimed it
winner of an Isthmian prize, because it had "won
in kicking." At this there was a general laugh and
uproar, while many applauded Diogenes and
derided the athletes. They say, too, that some
persons actually left without witnessing their
performances — those who had poor lodgings or
none.

Diogenes Laertius – Book 6.62

When a boy showed him a sword that [Diogenes]
had received from one to whom he had done
some discreditable service, he told him, "The
sword is a good sword, but the handle is
infamous."

Lucian – The Death of Peregrine 15

"Here is true philosophy; true patriotism; the
spirit of Diogenes and Crates is here!"

Diogenes Laertius – Book 6.30-31

And Eubulus[49] says, in his essay entitled, *The Sale
of Diogenes*, that [Diogenes] taught the children of
Xeniades, after their other lessons, to ride, and
shoot, and sling, and dart. And then in the
Gymnasium he did not permit the trainer to
exercise them after the fashion of athletes, but
exercised them himself to just the degree
sufficient to give them a good colour and good
health. And the boys retained in their memory
many sentences of poets and prose writers, and of
Diogenes himself; and he used to give them a
concise statement of everything in order to
strengthen their memory; and at home he used to
teach them to wait upon themselves, contenting
themselves with plain food, and drinking water.
And he accustomed them to cut their hair close,
and to eschew ornament, and to go without tunics
or shoes, and to keep silent, looking at nothing
except themselves as they walked along. He used,
also to take them out hunting; and they paid the

---

[49] An author

greatest attention and respect to Diogenes himself, and spoke well of him to their parents.

AUGUST 10

Diogenes Laertius – Book 6.56

[Diogenes] once begged of a covetous man, and as he was slow to give, he said, "Man, I am asking you for something to maintain me (eis trophen) and not to bury me (eis taphen)."

AUGUST 11

Tertullian – Against Marcion 1

For the cynic Diogenes used to go about, lantern in hand, at mid-day to find a man; whereas Marcion[50] has quenched the light of his faith, and so lost the God whom he had found.

AUGUST 12

Philo – Every Good Man is Free 121-126

And then, speaking boldly to someone who seemed inclined to become a purchaser, and who asked [Diogenes] the question, "What do you know?" he replied, "I know how to govern men:"

---

[50] An important figure in early Christianity. Marcion preached that the god who sent Jesus into the world was a different, higher deity than the creator god of Judaism.

his soul from within, as it appears, prompting his free, and noble, and naturally royal spirit. And then he at once, with his natural indifference and serenity, turned to facetious discourse, at which all the rest, who were all full of despondency were annoyed. Accordingly it is said that, seeing one of the intended purchasers afflicted with the female disease, as he did not even look like a man, he went up to him, and said, "Do you buy me, for you appear to me to be in want of a husband;" so that he, being grieved and downcast by reason of the infirmities of which he was conscious, slunk away, while all the rest admired the ready wit and happy courage of the philosopher. Shall we then say that such a man as this was in a state of slavery, and not rather in a state of freedom, only without any irresponsible authority? And there was also a man of the name of Choereas, a man of considerable education, who was a zealous imitator of Diogenes's freedom of speech; for he, being an inhabitant of Alexandria in Egypt, on one occasion, when Ptolemy was offended with him, and was uttering no slight threats against him, thinking that the freedom which was implanted in his nature was in no respect inferior to the royal authority of the other, replied– Rule your Egyptian slaves; but as for me, I neither care for you, nor fear your wrath and angry threats.

AUGUST 13

Philo – Every Good Man is Free 121-126

Accordingly the Cynic philosopher, Diogenes,
exhibited such a loftiness and greatness of spirit,
that when he was taken prisoner by some robbers,
and when they fed him very sparingly, and scarcely
gave him even necessary food, he was not weighed
down by the circumstances which surrounded
him, and did not fear the inhumanity of the
masters into whose power he had fallen, but said
"that it was a most absurd thing for pigs or sheep,
when they were going to be sold, to be carefully
provided with abundant food, so as to be
rendered fat and fleshy; but for the most excellent
of all animals, man, to be reduced to a skeleton by
bad food and continual scarcity, and so to be
rendered of less value than before."

AUGUST 14

Dio Chrysostom – Oration 72.10-11, 13, 16

And there are those who think that Aesop too was
somewhat like the Seven Sages, that while he was
wise and sensible, yet he was crafty too and clever
at composing tales such as they themselves would
most enjoy to hear. And possibly they are not
wholly mistaken in their suppositions and in
reality Aesop did in this way try to admonish
mankind and show them wherein they were in
error, believing that they would be most tolerant
toward him if they were amused by his humour
and his tales — just as children, when their nurses
tell them stories, not only pay attention to them
but are amused as well. As the result, then, of this

belief, that they are going to hear from us too
some such saying as Aesop used to utter, or
Socrates, or Diogenes, they draw near and annoy
and cannot leave in peace whomever they may see
in this costume, any more than the birds can when
they see an owl.

AUGUST 15

Diogenes Laertius – Book 6.38

On one occasion a man was reading some long
passages, and when he came to the end of the
book and showed that there was nothing more
written, "Be of good cheer, my friends,"
exclaimed Diogenes, "I see land."

AUGUST 16

Diogenes Laertius – Book 6.69

On one occasion [Diogenes] was asked, what was
the most excellent thing among men; and he said,
"Freedom of speech."

AUGUST 17

Dio Chrysostom – Fragments

"[Criticism]," Diogenes was wont to say, "is
another's blessing."

AUGUST 18

Greek Anthology – Anonymous

Diogenes the Cynic, on his arrival in Hades, after his wise old age was finished, laughed when he saw Croesus[51]. Spreading his cloak on the ground near the king, who once drew great store of gold from the river, he said: "Now, too, I take up more room than you; for all I had I have brought with me, but you, Croesus, have nothing."

AUGUST 19

Diogenes Laertius – Book 6.48

When Hegesias[52] entreated him to lend him one of his books, [Diogenes] said, "You are a silly fellow, Hegesias, for you will not take painted figs, but real ones; and yet you overlook the genuine practice of virtue, and seek for what is merely written."

AUGUST 20

Diogenes Laertius – Book 6.68

A man once said to him, that his friends laid plots

---

[51] King of Lydia who reigned until his defeat by the Persian king Cyrus the Great
[52] A Cyrenaic philosopher, who held the belief that happiness is unable to be obtained and death is an escape from pain and sorrow.

against him; "What then," said [Diogenes], "are
you to do, if you must look upon both your
friends and enemies in the same light?"

AUGUST 21

Diogenes Laertius – Book 6.38

And another of his sayings was that [Diogenes]
opposed confidence to fortune, nature to law, and
reason to suffering.

AUGUST 22

Socrates Scholasticus – Book 3.23

Because of [the Delphic] oracle Diogenes the
Cynic, and Oënomaus the Philosopher, strongly
condemned Apollo.

AUGUST 23

Diogenes Laertius – Book 6.87

Diocles relates how Diogenes persuaded Crates to
give up his fields to sheep pasture, and throw into
the sea any money he had.

AUGUST 24

Diogenes Laertius – Book 6.62

A counterfeit son (hupoleimaios) of somebody

once said to [Diogenes], that he had gold in his
cloak; "No doubt," said he, "that is the very
reason why I sleep with it under my head
(hupobeblemenos)."

AUGUST 25

Cicero, Tusculan Disputations, 5.92

But Diogenes took a greater liberty, like a Cynic,
when Alexander asked him if he wanted anything:
"Just at present," said he, "I wish that you would
stand a little out of the line between me and the
sun," for Alexander was hindering him from
sunning himself. And, indeed, this very man used
to maintain how much he surpassed the Persian
king in his manner of life and fortune; for that he
himself was in want of nothing, while the other
never had enough; and that he had no inclination
for those pleasures of which the other could never
get enough to satisfy himself; and that the other
could never obtain his.

AUGUST 26

Diogenes Laertius – Book 6.46

When [Diogenes] saw a young man going with
some satraps to supper, he dragged him away and
led him off to his relations, and bade them take
care of him.

AUGUST 27

Epictetus – Discourses 3.24

Go to, did Diogenes love no one, he who was so
gentle and kind-hearted that he cheerfully took
upon him all those troubles and distresses of body
for the general good of men? But how did he
love? As the servant of Zeus should love, caring
for his friends, but submitting himself to God.
That was why he alone made the whole world his
country, and no special land, and when he was
made prisoner he did not long for Athens or for
his friends and companions there, but made
himself at home with the pirates who took him
and tried to make them better, and afterwards
when he was sold he lived in Corinth just as he
lived before in Athens; yes, and if he had gone
away to the Perrhaebians[53] it would have been just
the same. That is how freedom is achieved. That is
why he said, "since Antisthenes freed me, I have
ceased to be a slave." How did he free him? Hear
what he says: "He taught me what is mine and
what is not mine; property is not mine; kinsfolk,
relations, friends, reputation, familiar places,
converse with men—none of these is my own."

AUGUST 28

---

[53] An ancient Greek people who lived in northern Thessaly.

Diogenes Laertius – Book 6.41

Once, when a man had struck him with his fist,
[Diogenes] said, "O Hercules, what a strange thing
that, I should be walking about with a helmet on
without knowing it!"

AUGUST 29

Lucian – Defense of the Portrait Study 17

You are an exact illustration of what Diogenes
said when someone asked him how he might
become famous:— "by despising fame."

AUGUST 30

Plutarch – Of the Tranquility of the Mind

Diogenes, when he was exposed to sale in the
market and was commanded to stand up, not only
refused to do it, but ridiculed the auctioneer, with
this piece of raillery: What! if you were selling a
fish, would you bid it rise up?

AUGUST 31

Diogenes Laertius – Book 6.47

He used to call the orators, and all those who
speak for fame triganthrôpoi (thrice men), instead
of trigathloi (thrice miserable).

SEPTEMBER

Clement, Stromata 7.4

Diogenes accordingly remarked well to one who
wondered at finding a serpent coiled round a
pestle: "Don"t wonder; for it would have been
more surprising if you had seen the pestle coiled
round the serpent, and the serpent straight." For
the irrational creatures must run, and scamper,
and fight, and breed, and die; and these things
being natural to them, can never be unnatural to
us. And many birds beneath the sunbeams walk.
And the comic poet Philemon treats such points
in comedy: — When I see one who watches who
has sneezed, Or who has spoke; or looking, who
goes on, I straightway in the market sell him off.
Each one of us walks, talks, and sneezes too, for
his own self, not for the citizens: According to
their nature things turn out. Then by the practice
of temperance men seek health: and by cramming
themselves, and wallowing in potations at feasts,
they attract diseases. There are many, too, that
dread inscriptions set up. Very cleverly Diogenes,
on finding in the house of a bad man the
inscription, "Hercules, for victory famed, dwells
here; let nothing bad enter," remarked, "And how
shall the master of the house go in?"

Julian – Oration 6

Now the founder of this philosophy to whom we are to attribute it, in the first instance, is not easy to discover, even though some think that the title belongs to Antisthenes and Diogenes. At least the saying of Oenomaus[54] seems to be not without good grounds: "The Cynic philosophy is neither Antisthenism nor Diogenism."

SEPTEMBER 3

Julian – Oration 6

And now, since it has become evident that Plato was not pursuing one aim and Diogenes another, but their end was one and the same; suppose one should inquire of the wise Plato: What value do you set on the precept "Know Thyself"? I am very sure that he would answer that it is worth everything, and indeed he says so in the *Alcibiades*. Come then tell us next, divine Plato, scion of the gods, how one ought to be disposed towards the opinions of the many? He will give the same answer, and moreover he will expressly enjoin on us to read his dialogue the *Crito*, where Socrates is shown warning us not to take heed of such things. At any rate what he says is: "But why, my dear good Crito, are we so concerned about the opinion of the multitude?" And now are we to ignore all this evidence, and without further question fence off from one another and force

---

[54] A Cynic philosopher. He is known principally for the long extracts of a work attacking oracles.

apart men whom the passion for truth, the scorn
of opinion, and unanimity in zeal for virtue have
joined together? And if Plato chose to achieve his
aim through words, whereas for Diogenes deeds
sufficed, does the latter on that account deserve to
be criticised by you? Nay, consider whether that
same method of his be not in every respect
superior; since we see that Plato for himself
forswore written compositions. "For", he says,
"there are no writings by Plato nor ever will be,
and what now pass current as his are the work of
Socrates, the ever fair and fever young." Why then
should we not from the practice of Diogenes
study the character of the Cynic philosophy?

SEPTEMBER 4

Diogenes Laertius – Book 6.33

[Diogenes] used to call anaperoi (cripples), not
those who were dumb and blind, but those who
had no wallet (pera).

SEPTEMBER 5

Diogenes Laertius – Book 6.29

And so [Diogenes] bade the crier "give notice that
if anyone wants to purchase a master, there is one
here for him."

SEPTEMBER 6

Diogenes Laertius – Book 6.70

[Diogenes] used to say, that there were two kinds
of exercise: that, namely, of the mind and that of
the body; and that the latter of these created in the
mind such quick and agile phantasies at the time
of its performance, as very much facilitated the
practice of virtue; but that one was imperfect
without the other, since the health and vigour
necessary for the practice of what is good, depend
equally on both mind and body.

SEPTEMBER 7

Diogenes Laertius – Book 6.22

[Diogenes] saw a mouse running about and not
seeking for a bed, nor taking care to keep in the
dark, nor looking for any of those things which
appear enjoyable to such an animal, he found a
remedy for his own poverty.

SEPTEMBER 8

Diogenes Laertius – Book 6.48

And when a man, who was very superstitious, said
to [Diogenes], "With one blow I will break your
head;" "And I," he replied, "with one sneeze will
make you tremble."

SEPTEMBER 9

Diogenes Laertius – Book 6.34

On one occasion [Diogenes] found Demosthenes,
the orator, dining in an inn; and as he was slipping
away, he said to him, "You will now be ever so
much more in an inn."

SEPTEMBER 10

Plutarch – Of Eating of Flesh 1.6

Diogenes ventured once to eat a raw octopus, that
he might disuse himself from meat dressed by fire;
and as several priests and other people stood
round him, he wrapped his head in his cloak, and
so putting the fish to his mouth, he thus said unto
them: It is for your sake, sirs, that I undergo this
danger, and run this risk.

SEPTEMBER 11

Diogenes Laertius – Book 6.43

He was greatly beloved by the Athenians;
accordingly, when a youth had broken his [tub],
[the Athenians] beat him, and gave Diogenes
another.

SEPTEMBER 12

Julian – Oration 6

For Diogenes possessed nothing that is usually

offered, incense or libations or money to buy
them with. But if he held right opinions about the
gods, that in itself was enough. For he worshipped
them with his whole soul, thus offering them as I
think the most precious of his possessions, the
dedication of his soul through his thoughts.

SEPTEMBER 13

Diogenes Laertius – Book 6.69

[Diogenes] was in the habit of doing everything in
public, whether in respect of [Aphrodite] or
[Demeter]; and he used to put his conclusions in
this way to people: "If there is nothing absurd in
dining, then it is not absurd to dine in the market-
place. But it is not absurd to dine, therefore it is
not absurd to dine in the market-place."

SEPTEMBER 14

Julian – Oration 6

Now consider whether Diogenes did not above all
other men profess this belief, since he freely
exposed his body to hardships so that he might
make it stronger than it was by nature. He allowed
himself to act only as the light of reason shows us
that we ought to act; and the perturbations that
attack the soul and are derived from the body, to
which this envelope of ours often constrains us
for its sake to pay too much attention, he did not
take into account at all. Thus by means of this

discipline the man made his body more vigorous, I
believe, than that of any who have contended for
the prize of a crown in the games; and his soul
was so disposed that he was happy and a king no
less if not even more than the Great King, as the
Greeks used to call him in those days, by which
they meant the king of Persia. Then does he seem
to you of no importance, this man who was
"cityless, homeless, a man without a country,
owning not an obol, not a drachma, not a single
slave," nay, not even a loaf of bread and Epicurus[55]
says that if he have bread enough and to spare he
is not inferior to the gods on the score of
happiness.

SEPTEMBER 15

Athenaeus – Deipnosophistae Book 4.158.f

And Socrates used to say that he differed from all
other men in that they live to eat whereas he ate to
live. Diogenes, too, answered those who chided
him for rubbing himself down: "Would that I
were able, by rubbing my belly as well, to quell its
hunger and want!"

SEPTEMBER 16

Diogenes Laertius – Book 6.6

---

[55] An ancient Greek philosopher and sage who founded
Epicureanism, a highly influential school of philosophy.

When Diogenes begged a coat of him, he bade
him fold his cloak around him double.

SEPTEMBER 17

Diogenes Laertius – Book 6.82

Monimus of Syracuse[56] was a pupil of Diogenes;
and, according to Sosicrates, he was in the service
of a certain Corinthian banker, to whom
Xeniades, the purchaser of Diogenes, made
frequent visits, and by the account which he gave
of his goodness in word and deed, excited in
Monimus a passionate admiration of Diogenes.
For he forthwith pretended to be mad and
proceeded to fling away the small change and all
the money on the banker's table, until at length his
master dismissed him; and he then straightway
devoted himself to Diogenes.

SEPTEMBER 18

Diogenes Laertius – Book 6.29

[Diogenes] would frequently praise those who
were about to marry, and yet did not marry; or
who were about to take a voyage, and yet did not
take a voyage; or who were about to engage in
affairs of state, and did not do so; and those who
were about to rear children, yet did not rear any;

---

[56] A Cynic philosopher who endorsed philosophical skepticism,
denying that there was a criterion of truth.

and those who were preparing to take up their
abode with princes, and yet did not take it up.
One of his sayings was, "That one ought to hold
out one's hand to a friend without closing the
fingers."

SEPTEMBER 19

Diogenes Laertius – Book 6.57

On one occasion, [Diogenes] saw a man who had
been detected stealing purple, and so he said, "A
purple death, and mighty fate overtook him".

SEPTEMBER 20

Diogenes Laertius – Book 6.35

When someone had dropped a loaf, and was
ashamed to pick it up again, [Diogenes], wishing
to give him a lesson, tied a cord round the neck of
a bottle and dragged it all through the Ceramicus[57].

SEPTEMBER 21

Diogenes Laertius – Book 6.51

---

[57] An extensive area both within and outside the ancient city walls, on
both sides of the Dipylon Gate and by the banks of the Eridanos
River. It was the potters' quarter of the city, from which the English
word "ceramic" is derived, and was also the site of an important
cemetery and numerous funerary sculptures erected along the road
out of the city towards Eleusis.

Having heard once that Didymon[58] the adulterer,
had been caught in the fact, [Diogenes] said, "He
deserves to be hung by his name."

SEPTEMBER 22

Diogenes Laertius – Book 6.66

Being once reproached for drinking in a [tavern],
[Diogenes] said, "I have my hair cut, too, in a
barber's."

SEPTEMBER 23

Diogenes Laertius – Book 6.64

A man once brought him a boy, and said that he
was a very clever child, and one of [excellent
character]." "What, then," said Diogenes, "does
he want of me?"

SEPTEMBER 24

Diogenes Laertius – Book 6.44

When Perdiccas[59] threatened that he would put
him to death if he did not come to him,

---

[58] The "twin".
[59] A general in Alexander the Great's army and participated in
Alexander's campaign against Persia. Following Alexander's death, he
rose to become supreme commander of the imperial army and
regent.

[Diogenes] replied, "That is nothing strange, for a scorpion or a tarantula could do as much: you had better threaten me that, if I kept away, you should be very happy."

SEPTEMBER 25

Diogenes Laertius – Book 6.54

When asked what wine he liked to drink, [Diogenes] said, "That which belongs to another,"

SEPTEMBER 26

Diogenes Laertius – Book 6.55

When he was dining on olives, a cheese-cake was brought in, on which he threw the olive away, saying: "Keep well aloof, O stranger, from all tyrants".

SEPTEMBER 27

Diogenes Laertius – Book 6.71

[Diogenes] said: For the very contempt of pleasure, if we only inure ourselves to it, is very pleasant; and just as they who are accustomed to live luxuriously, are brought very unwillingly to adopt the contrary system; so they who have been originally inured to that opposite system, feel a sort of pleasure in the contempt of pleasure.

SEPTEMBER 28

Diogenes Laertius – Book 6.65

Seeing a handsome young man chattering in an unseemly manner, [Diogenes] said, "Are you not ashamed to draw a sword cut of lead out of a scabbard of ivory?"

SEPTEMBER 29

Diogenes Laertius – Book 6.66

One of [Diogenes'] sayings was, that servants serve their masters, and that wicked men are the slaves of their appetites.

SEPTEMBER 30

Diogenes Laertius – Book 6.34

[Diogenes] used to go bare foot through the snow.

,

OCTOBER

OCTOBER 1

Plutarch – The Remarkable Speeches of Some
Obscure Men Amongst the Spartans 1

Another Spartan, seeing Diogenes the Cynic in
very cold weather embrace a brazen statue, asked
whether he was not very cold; and he replying,
No, he rejoined, What great matter then is it that
you do?

OCTOBER 2

Diogenes Laertius – Book 6.63

When a man reproached [Diogenes] for going into
unclean places, he said, "The sun too penetrates
into toilets, but is not polluted by them."

OCTOBER 3

Plutarch – Life of Timoleon 15

Now, Plato did not live to see Dionysius when he
was in Corinth, but he was already dead; Diogenes
of Sinope, however, on meeting him for the first
time, said: "How little though deservest,
Dionysius, thus to live!" Upon this, Dionysius
stopped and said: "It is good of thee, O Diogenes,
to sympathize with me in my misfortunes." "How
is that?" said Diogenes; "Dost thou suppose that I
am sympathizing with thee? Nay, I am indignant
that such a slave as thou, and one so worthy to

have grown old and died in the tyrant's estate, just
as thy father did, should be living here with us in
mirth and luxury."

OCTOBER 4

Diogenes Laertius – Book 6.24

[Diogenes] was very violent in expressing his
haughty disdain of others.

OCTOBER 5

Aelian – Varia Historia 3.29 — Of the Poverty
and Pride of Diogenes

Diogenes the Sinopean used to say of himself, that
he fulfilled and suffered the imprecations
mentioned in the tragedy, being a vagabond,
destitute of a house, deprived of his country, a
beggar, ill clothed, having his livelihood only from
day to day: And yet he was more pleased with this
condition, then Alexander with the command of
the whole world, when having conquered the
Indians he returned to Babylon.

OCTOBER 6

Diogenes Laertius – Book 6.42

Once [Diogenes] saw a man purifying himself by
washing, and said to him, "Oh, wretched man, do
not you know that as you cannot wash away

blunders in grammar by purification, so, too, you can no more efface the errors of a life in that same manner?"

OCTOBER 7

Athenaeus – Deipnosophistae Book 6

Concerning this city Diogenes was right in saying that it had far better go to the vultures rather than to the flatterers, for the latter devour good men while they are still alive.

OCTOBER 8

Diogenes Laertius – Book 6.34

When some people said to [Diogenes], "You are an old man, and should rest for the remainder of your life;" "Why so?" replied he, "suppose I had run a long distance, ought I to stop when I was near the end, and not rather press on?"

OCTOBER 9

Diogenes Laertius – Book 6.27

When [Diogenes] was asked where in Greece he saw virtuous men; "Men," said he, "nowhere; but I see good boys in Lacedaemon."

OCTOBER 10

Epictetus – Discourses 1.24

Diogenes, who was sent scouting before you, has
brought us back a different report: he says,
"Death is not evil, for it is not dishonour"; he
says, "Glory is a vain noise made by madmen".
And what a message this scout brought us about
pain and pleasure and poverty! "To wear no
raiment", he says, "is better than any robe with
purple hem"; "to sleep on the ground without a
bed", he says, "is the softest couch." Moreover he
proves each point by showing his own confidence,
his tranquillity of mind, his freedom, and withal
his body well knit, and in good condition. "No
enemy is near," he says, "all is full of peace." What
do you mean, Diogenes? "see," he says, "have I
suffered shot or wound or rout?" That is the right
kind of scouting: but you come back to us and talk
at random. Drop your cowardice and go back
again, and take a more accurate observation.

OCTOBER 11

Julian – Oration 9.256

According to Diogenes "The man without a city,
without a home, bereft of a fatherland," that is to
say, a man who can gain nothing from Fortune,
and on the other hand has nothing to lose.

OCTOBER 12

Diogenes Laertius – Book 6.61

Once [Diogenes] saw a man who had been a
conqueror at the Olympic games looking very
often at a courtesan; "Look" said he, "at that
warlike ram, who is taken prisoner by the first girl
he meets."

OCTOBER 13

Diogenes Laertius – Book 6.62

Seeing an unskillful wrestler professing to heal a
man [Diogenes] said, "What are you about, are
you in hopes now to overthrow those who
formerly conquered you?"

OCTOBER 14

Diogenes Laertius – Book 6.54

Once [Diogenes] saw a youth blushing, and
addressed him, "Courage, my boy, that is the
complexion of virtue."

OCTOBER 15

Diogenes Laertius – Book 6.65

When [Diogenes] saw an ignorant man tuning a
psaltery, he said to him, "Are you not ashamed to
be arranging proper sounds on a wooden

instrument, and not arranging your soul to a
proper life?"

OCTOBER 16

Diogenes Laertius – Book 6.51

When [Diogenes] saw a woman in a litter, he said,
"The cage is not suited to the animal."

OCTOBER 17

Philostratus –Life of Apollonius 7.2

Then there were Diogenes of Sinope and Crates
of Thebes, of whom the former went direct to
Chaeronea, and rebuked Philip for his treatment
of the Athenians, on the ground that, though
asserting himself to be a descendant of Heracles
he yet was destroying by force of arms those who
had taken up arms in defense of the descendants
of Heracles.

OCTOBER 18

Diogenes Laertius – Book 6.64

Once [Diogenes] was going into a theatre while
everyone else was coming out of it; and when
asked why he did so, "It is," said he, "what I have
been doing all my life."

OCTOBER 19

Diogenes Laertius – Book 6.46

When [Diogenes] was in want of money, he said that he reclaimed it from his friends and did not beg for it.

OCTOBER 20

Jerome – Against Jovinian 2.14

Satyrus[60], the biographer of illustrious men, relates that Diogenes to guard himself against the cold, folded his cloak double: his scrip was his pantry: and when aged he carried a stick to support his feeble frame, and was commonly called Old Hand-to-mouth, because to that very hour he begged and received food from any one.

OCTOBER 21

Julian – Oration 6

On the other hand when Diogenes made unseemly noises or obeyed the call of nature or did anything else of that sort in the market-place, as they say he did, he did so because he was trying to trample on the conceit of the men I have just mentioned, and to teach them that their practices

---

[60] A distinguished peripatetic philosopher and historian.

were far more sordid and insupportable than his
own. For what he did was in accordance with the
nature of all of us, but theirs accorded with no
man's real nature, one may say, but were all due to
moral depravity.

OCTOBER 22

Diogenes Laertius – Book 6.40

When Plato called him a dog, he said,
"Undoubtedly, for I have come back to those who
sold me."

OCTOBER 23

Diogenes Laertius – Book 6.47

To a young man who was complaining of the
number of people who sought his acquaintance,
[Diogenes] said, "Do not make such a parade of
your vanity."

OCTOBER 24

Diogenes Laertius – Book 6.38

Once, while [Diogenes] was sitting in the sun in
the Craneum[61], Alexander was standing by, and
said to him, "Ask any favour you choose of me."

---

[61] A grove of cypresses near Corinth used as a gymnasium.

And he replied, "Cease to shade me from the sun."

OCTOBER 25

Diogenes Laertius – Book 6.39

When the Athenians entreated [Diogenes] to be initiated in the Eleusinian mysteries[62], and said that in the shades below the initiated had the best seats; "It will," he replied, "be an absurd thing if Aegesilaus and Epaminondas[63] are to live in the mud, and some miserable wretches, who have been initiated, are to be in the islands of the blest."

OCTOBER 26

Plutarch – Concerning the Cure of Anger

But must rather take to himself the saying of Diogenes, who, when one said to him, They deride thee, O Diogenes, made answer, But I am not derided; and he must not think himself contemned, but rather himself contemn that man that offends him, as one acting out of weakness or

---

[62] The Eleusinian Mysteries were initiations held every year for the cult of Demeter and Persephone based at Eleusis in ancient Greece.
[63] Aegesilaus - Spartan king and general during the Corinthian War. He was widely admired throughout Greece. Epaminandas - A Greek general of Thebes and statesman of the 4th century BC who transformed the Ancient Greek city-state of Thebes, leading it out of Spartan subjugation into a pre-eminent position in Greek politics.

error, rashness or carelessness, rudeness or dotage,
or childishness.

OCTOBER 27

Diogenes Laertius – Book 6.30

When Xeniades bought him, [Diogenes] said to
him that he ought to obey him even though he
was his slave; for that a physician or a pilot would
find men to obey them even though they might be
slaves.

OCTOBER 28

Jerome – Against Jovinian 2.14

[Diogenes] had a wooden dish for drinking; but
on one occasion seeing a boy drinking with the
hollow of his hand he is related to have dashed
the cup to the ground, saying that he did not
know nature provided a cup.

OCTOBER 29

Diogenes Laertius – Book 6.52

Another time, [Diogenes] saw a little boy who was
a stealer of clothes from the baths, and said, "Are
you going for perfumes, (aleimmation), or for
other garments (all" himation).

OCTOBER 30

Diogenes Laertius – Book 6.63

[Diogenes] said: "spoil all the rest, but keep your hands from Hector."

OCTOBER 31

Diogenes Laertius – Book 6.34

Once, when [Diogenes] was invited to a banquet, he said that he would not come: for that the day before no one had thanked him for coming.

NOVEMBER

NOVEMBER 1

Lucian – Dialogues of the Dead excerpts

Diogenes. Equals! My dear sir, no; I don"t say that. While Mausolus is groaning over the memories of earth, and the felicity which he supposed to be his, Diogenes will be chuckling. While Mausolus boasts of the tomb raised to him by Artemisia[64], his wife and sister, Diogenes knows not whether he has a tomb or no — the question never having occurred to him; he knows only that his name is on the tongues of the wise, as one who lived the life of a man; a higher monument than yours, vile Carian[65] slave, and set on firmer foundations.

NOVEMBER 2

Diogenes Laertius – Book 6.63

When [Diogenes] was asked what advantage he had derived from philosophy, he replied, "If no other, at least this, that I am prepared for every kind of fortune."

NOVEMBER 3

---

[64] Artemisia - Wife and sister of Mausolus. She finished his famous mausoleum.
[65] Ancient inhabitants of Caria in southwest Anatolia, modern Turkey

Diogenes Laertius – Book 6.60

When Phryne[66] had dedicated a golden statue of
[Aphrodite] at Delphi, he wrote upon it, "From
the profligacy of the Greeks."

NOVEMBER 4

Diogenes Laertius – Book 6.72

And [Diogenes] used to argue thus, —
"Everything belongs to the gods; and wise men
are the friends of the gods. All things are in
common among friends; therefore everything
belongs to wise men."

NOVEMBER 5

Aesop 85 – Diogenes and the Ferryman

On his travels, Diogenes the Cynic came to a
stream that was flooded. He stood on the bank,
unable to go any farther. One of those ferrymen
who regularly carry people across rivers saw that
Diogenes did not know what to do so he
approached the philosopher, picked him up, and
kindly carried him across the water. Diogenes then
stood on the opposite shore, bewailing the
poverty that prevented him from rewarding the
man for his good deed. While Diogenes was still

---

[66] An ancient Greek courtesan (hetaira), from the fourth century BC.
She is best known for her trial for impiety.

pondering this state of affairs, the ferryman saw
another traveller who could not get across, so he
ran off to offer his assistance. Diogenes accosted
the ferryman and said, "Well, I do not feel in your
debt any longer for the favour that you did me.
This is not an act of judgment on your part — it's
an addiction!" The story shows that someone who
assists both the truly good and those who are
undeserving is not seen as a philanthropist, but is
instead regarded as a madman.

NOVEMBER 6

Athenaeus – Deipnosophistae Book 2.49.a-b

When a Cynic called the four-legged table a tripod,
one of the guests at the savant's dinner, took
exception and said: "Today "I am going to have
business on my hands after a period of idleness."
For where does he get his word "tripod"?...unless,
of course, he counts Diogenes' staff along with his
legs and calls him a tripod, when everybody else
call what are here set before us four-legged
tables."

NOVEMBER 7

Plutarch – Of Bashfulness

Diogenes went about begging to all the statues in
the Ceramicus; and his answer to some that
wondered at his fancy in it was, he was practising
how to bear a repulse.

NOVEMBER 8

Diogenes Laertius – Book 6.50

On one occasion, [Diogenes] was asked by the tyrant, "What sort of brass was the best, for a statue?" and he replied, "That of which the statues of Harmodius and Aristogiton[67] are made."

NOVEMBER 9

Seneca – Epistle 29

[Not being afraid to offer the truth] is why it is often doubted whether Diogenes and the other Cynics, who employed an undiscriminating freedom of speech and offered advice to any who came in their way, ought to have pursued such a plan.

NOVEMBER 10

Diogenes Laertius – Book 6.47

When [Diogenes] saw a notice on the house of a

---

[67] Two lovers from ancient Athens. They became known as the Tyrannicides (τυραννόκτονοι, tyrannoktonoi), the preeminent symbol of democracy to ancient Athenians, after they committed an act of political assassination at the 514 BC Panathenaic Festival. They assassinated Hipparchus, thought to be the last Peisistratid tyrant, though according to Thucydides Hipparchus was not a tyrant but a minister. They also planned to kill the real tyrant of Athens, Hippias, but were unsuccessful.

profligate man, "To be sold." "I knew," said he,
"that you who are so incessantly drunk, would
soon vomit up your owner."

NOVEMBER 11

Diogenes Laertius – Book 6.23

Being attacked with illness, [Diogenes] supported
himself with a staff; and after that he carried it
continually, not indeed in the city, but whenever
he was walking in the roads, together with his
wallet.

NOVEMBER 12

Diogenes Laertius – Book 6.68

[Diogenes] used to say, that education was, for the
young sobriety, for the old comfort, for the poor
riches, and for the rich an ornament.

NOVEMBER 13

Lucian – The True History Book 2.18

[In Lucian's upside-down satire.] Diogenes of
Sinope was much changed; he had married Lais[68]

---

[68] A famous hetaira or courtesan of ancient Greece who was probably
born in Corinth.

the courtesan, and often in his cups would oblige
the company with a dance, or other mad pranks.

NOVEMBER 14

Diogenes Laertius – Book 6.68

When Alexander was once standing by him, and
saying, "Do not you fear me?" He replied, "No;
for what are you, a good or an evil?" And as he
said that he was good, "Who, then," said
Diogenes, "fears the good?"

NOVEMBER 15

Strabo – Geography 15.65

At all events, all he said, according to Onesicritus,
tended to this, that the best teaching is that which
removes pleasure and pain from the soul; and that
pain and toil differ, for the former is inimical to
man and the latter friendly, since man trains the
body for toil in order that his opinions may be
strengthened, whereby he may put a stop to
dissensions and be ready to give good advice to
all, both in public and in private; and that,
furthermore, he had now advised Taxiles[69] to
receive Alexander, for if he received a man better
than himself he would be well treated, but if

---

[69] The Greek chroniclers' name for a prince or king who reigned over
the tract between the Indus and the Jhelum (Hydaspes) Rivers in the
Punjab region of India.

inferior, he would improve him. Onesicritus[70] says that, after saying this, Mandanis[71] inquired whether such doctrines were taught among the Greeks; and that when he answered that Pythagoras[72] taught such doctrines, and also bade people to abstain from meat, as did also Socrates and Diogenes, and that he himself had been a pupil of Diogenes, Mandanis replied that he regarded the Greeks as sound-minded if, but that they were wrong in one respect, in that they preferred custom to nature; for otherwise, Mandanis said, they would not be ashamed to go naked, like himself, and live on frugal fare; for, he added, the best house is that which requires the least repairs.

NOVEMBER 16

Aelian – Varia Historia 4.11 — Of the Luxury of Socrates

Diogenes said that Socrates himself was luxurious: for he was too curious in his little house, and in his little bed, and in the sandals which he used to wear.

---

[70] A Greek historical writer and Cynic philosopher, who accompanied Alexander the Great on his campaigns in Asia.

[71] A gymnosophist, of "naked teacher", who was encountered in Alexander's conquest of India

[72] A famous philosopher of the 6th century BCE, founded a school in which initiates were sworn to secrecy and lived a communal, ascetic lifestyle. This lifestyle entailed a number of dietary prohibitions, traditionally said to have included vegetarianism,

NOVEMBER 17

Diogenes Laertius – Book 6.66

A man once struck him with a beam, and then
said, "Take care." "What," said [Diogenes], "are
you going to strike me again?"

NOVEMBER 18

Diogenes Laertius – Book 6.33

A man once said to [Diogenes], "I conquered men
at the Pythian Games[73]:" on which he said, "I
conquer men, but you only conquer slaves."

NOVEMBER 19

Theophilus – Letter to Autolycus 3.5

Philosophers Inculcate Cannibalism. Since, then,
you have read much, what is your opinion of the
precepts of Zeno, and Diogenes, and Cleanthes[74],
which their books contain, inculcating the eating
of human flesh: that fathers be cooked and eaten
by their own children; and that if anyone refuse or

---

[73] One of the four Panhellenic Games of Ancient Greece. They were
held in honour of Apollo following the quadrennial (quinquennial in
the ancient way of numbering) chronology of the Olympic Games, at
his sanctuary at Delphi.
[74] Zeno was the founder of the Stoic school of philosophy, and
Cleanthes was his successor. Both advocated ethical positions similar
to Cynicism.

reject a part of this infamous food, he himself be
devoured who will riot eat? An utterance even
more godless than these is found—that, namely,
of Diogenes, who teaches children to bring their
own parents in sacrifice, and devour them.

NOVEMBER 20

Diogenes Laertius – Book 6.63

When the Athenians had voted that Alexander
was Bacchus, [Diogenes] said to them, "Vote, too,
that I am Serapis[75]."

NOVEMBER 21

Aelian – Varia Historia 13.26 — How Diogenes in
extreme indigence comforted himself

Diogenes the Sinopean was left alone deserted by
all men, not being able by reason of his indigence
to entertain any man, nor would anyone entertain
him, all avoiding him because of his sower way of
reprehension, and because he was morose in all
his actions and sayings. Hereupon he became
troubled, and did feed on the tops of leaves; for

---

[75] Serapis was depicted as Greek in appearance but with Egyptian
trappings, and combined iconography from a great many cults,
signifying both abundance and resurrection. Serapis was a syncretistic
deity derived from the worship of the Egyptian Osiris and Apis and
also gained attributes from other deities, such as chthonic powers
linked to the Greek Hades and Demeter, and benevolence linked to
Dionysus.

this food was ready for him. But a mouse coming thither, fed upon some crumbs of bread which she found scattered there; which Diogenes diligently observing, smiled, and becoming more cheerful and pleasant to himself said; "This mouse requires not the plentiful diet of the Athenians, and art thou Diogenes troubled that thou dost not feast with them?" By this means he acquired tranquility to himself.

NOVEMBER 22

Diogenes Laertius – Book 6.71

This used to be the language which [Diogenes] held, and he used to show in practice, really altering men's habits, and deferring in all things rather to the principles of nature than to those of law; saying that he was adopting the same fashion of life as Heracles had, preferring nothing in the world to liberty.

NOVEMBER 23

Julian – Oration 6

At any rate when Antisthenes was suffering from a long and incurable illness Diogenes handed him a dagger with these words, "In case you need the aid of a friend." So convinced was he that there is nothing terrible or grievous in death. But we who have inherited his staff know out of our greater wisdom that death is a calamity.

NOVEMBER 24

Diogenes Laertius – Book 6.18-19

When Diogenes offered [Aristotle] dried figs, he saw that he had prepared something caustic to say if he did not take them; so he took them and said Diogenes had lost his figs and his jest into the bargain.

NOVEMBER 25

Diogenes Laertius – Book 6.50

A man who was lately married put an inscription on his house, "Heracles Callinicus[76], the son of [Zeus], lives here; let no evil enter." And so Diogenes wrote in addition, "An alliance is made after the war is over."

NOVEMBER 26

Aelian – Varia Historia 12.58 — Dioxippus the Athenian, an Olympic Victor in Wrestling, was brought [in a Chariot]

In Athens, according to the custom of wrestlers. The multitude flocked together, and crowded to behold him. Amongst these a woman of extraordinary beauty came to see the Show.

---

[76] Hercules the "Victorious".

Dioxippus[77] beholding her, was immediately
overcome with her beauty, and looked fixedly
upon her, and turned his head back, often
changing colour, whereby he was plainly detected
by the people to be taken extraordinarily with the
woman. But Diogenes the Sinopean did chiefly
reprehend his passion thus; A gold tablet of
Corinthian work being set to sale, "Behold, said
he, your great wrestler with his neck writhed about
by a girl."

NOVEMBER 27

Diogenes Laertius – Book 6.44

[Diogenes] used constantly to repeat with
emphasis that an easy life had been given to man
by the Gods, but that it had been overlaid by their
seeking for honey, cheese-cakes, and unguents,
and things of that sort.

NOVEMBER 28

Diogenes Laertius – Book 6.39

A man once proved to him syllogistically that he
had horns, so [Diogenes] put his hand to his
forehead and said, "I do not see them."

---

[77] An ancient Greek pankratiast, renowned for his Olympic victories
in the sport of pankration.

Epictetus – Discourses 3.26

What you really fear is that you may not be able to
live the life of an invalid; for the life of healthy
men you have only to see how slaves and
labourers and true philosophers live; the life of
Socrates, though he had a wife and children to live
with, the life of Diogenes, and of Cleanthes, who
combined philosophy with drawing water. If this
is what you want to have, you will have it
everywhere, and will live with confidence.
Confidence in what? In that which alone it is
possible to confide in, what is trustworthy, and
cannot be hindered or taken away, that is, your
own will. Why have you made yourself so useless
and unprofitable that no one is willing to take you
into his house and take care of you? Everyone will
pick up a vessel that is whole and fit for use if it is
flung aside and will count it gain; but everyone will
count you loss, not gain. Cannot you even serve
the purpose of a dog or a rooster? Why then do
you wish to live any more, if this is your character?

Diogenes Laertius – Book 6.103-105

When somebody showed Diogenes a clock, he
pronounced it a serviceable instrument to save
one from being late for dinner. Again, to a man
who gave a musical recital before him he said: By

men's minds states are ordered well, and
households, not by the lyre's twanged strings or
flute's trilled notes.

DECEMBER

DECEMBER 1

Diogenes Laertius – Book 6.58

Some authors also attribute the following repartee
to [Aristippus]. Plato saw him washing vegetables,
and so, coming up to him, he quietly accosted him
thus, "If you had paid court to Dionysius you
would not have been washing vegetables." "And,"
he replied, with equal quietness, "if you had
washed vegetables, you would never have paid
court to Dionysius."

DECEMBER 2

Diogenes Laertius – Book 2.72

When [Aristippus] was reproached for employing
a rhetorician to conduct his case, he made reply,
"Well, if I give a dinner, I hire a cook."

DECEMBER 3

Plutarch – On Tranquility of Mind, 8

For most men leave the pleasant and delectable
things behind them, and run with haste to
embrace those which are not only difficult but
intolerable. Aristippus was not of this number, for
he knew, even to the niceness of a grain, to put
prosperous against adverse fortune into the scale,
that the one might outweigh the other. Therefore
when he lost a noble farm, he asked one of his

dissembled friends, who pretended to be sorry,
not only with regret but impatience, for his
mishap: "[You have] but one piece of land, but
have I not three farms yet remaining?" He
assenting to the truth of it: "Why then, [he said],
should I not rather lament your misfortune, since
it is the raving only of a mad man to be concerned
at what is lost, and not rather rejoice in what is
left?"

DECEMBER 4

Clement of Alexandria – Pedagogy 2.8

I know, too, the words of Aristippus the Cyrenian.
Aristippus was a luxurious man. He asked an
answer to a sophistical proposition in the
following terms: "A horse anointed with ointment
is not injured in his excellence as a horse, nor is a
dog which has been anointed, in his excellence as
a dog; no more is a man," he added, and so
finished.

DECEMBER 5

Athenaeus – Deipnosophistae Book 12

We find also whole schools of philosophers which
have openly professed to have made choice of
pleasure. And there is the school called the
Cyrenaic, which derives its origin from Aristippus
the pupil of Socrates: and he devoted himself to
pleasure in such a way, that he said that it was the

main end of life; and that happiness was founded
on it, and that happiness was at best but short-
lived. And he, like the most debauched of men,
thought that he had nothing to do either with the
recollection of past enjoyments, or with the hope
of future ones; but he judged of all good by the
present alone, and thought that having enjoyed,
and being about to enjoy, did not at all concern
him; since the one case had no longer any
existence, and the other did not yet exist and was
necessarily uncertain: acting in this respect like
thoroughly dissolute men, who are content with
being prosperous at the present moment. And his
life was quite consistent with his theory; for he
spent the whole of it in all kinds of luxury and
extravagance, both in perfumes, and dress, and
women. Accordingly, he openly kept Lais as his
mistress; and he delighted in all the extravagance
of Dionysius, although he was often treated
insultingly by him.

DECEMBER 6

Diogenes Laertius – Book 2.79

[Aristippus] was once staying in Asia and was
taken prisoner by Artaphernes, the satrap[78]. "Can
you be cheerful under these circumstances?"
someone asked. "Yes, you simpleton," was the
reply, "for when should I be more cheerful than

[78] A brother of the Achaemenid king of Persia, Darius I, satrap of
Lydia from the capital of Sardis, and a Persian general.

now that I am about to converse with Artaphernes
[having learned that from Socrates]?"

Aristotle – Rhetoric 2.23.11

Or again as Aristippus said in reply to Plato when
he spoke somewhat too dogmatically, as
Aristippus thought: "Well, anyhow, our friend",
meaning Socrates, "never spoke like that".

Athenaeus – Deipnosophistae Book 13

But Lais was so beautiful, that painters used to
come to her to copy her bosom and her breasts.
And Lais was a rival of Phryne, and had an
immense number of lovers, never caring whether
they were rich or poor, and never treating them
with any insolence. And Aristippus every year
used to spend whole days with her in Aegina, at
the festival of Poseidon. And once, being
reproached by his servant, who said to him, "You
give her such large sums of money, but she admits
Diogenes the Cynic for nothing". He answered, "I
give Lais a great deal, that I myself may enjoy her,
and not that no one else may." And when
Diogenes said, "since you, Aristippus, cohabit
with a common prostitute, either, therefore,
become a Cynic yourself, as I am, or else abandon
her". Aristippus answered him, "Does it appear to

you, Diogenes, an absurd thing to live in a house
where other men have lived before you?" "Not at
all," said he. "Well, then, does it appear to you
absurd to sail in a ship in which other men have
sailed before you?" "By no means," said he. "Well,
then," replied Aristippus, "it is not a bit more
absurd to be in love with a woman with whom
many men have been in love already."

DECEMBER 9

Plutarch – On Love 49

As Aristippus testified to one that would have put
him out of conceit with Lais, for that, as he said,
she did not truly love him; no more, said he, am I
beloved by pure wine or good fish, and yet I
willingly make use of both.

DECEMBER 10

Vitruvius – On Architecture, 6.1.1

It is related of the Socratic philosopher Aristippus
that, being shipwrecked and cast ashore on the
coast of the Rhodians, he observed geometrical
figures drawn thereon, and cried out to his
companions: "Let us be of good cheer, for I see
the traces of man." With that he made for the city
of Rhodes, and went straight to the gymnasium.
There he fell to discussing philosophical subjects,
and presents were bestowed upon him, so that he
could not only fit himself out, but could also

provide those who accompanied him with
clothing and all other necessaries of life. When his
companions wished to return to their country, and
asked him what message he wished them to carry
home, he bade them say this: that children ought
to be provided with property and resources of a
kind that could swim with them even out of a
shipwreck.

DECEMBER 11

Dio Chrysostom – The Tenth Discourse –
Diogenes, or On Servants

Diogenes answered, "by keeping him in idleness
and ignorance and making him as bad as could be?
For idleness and lack of occupation are the best
things in the world to ruin the foolish. Therefore
he was right in deciding that you were his
undoing, and he was justified in running off,
evidently so as to get work and not become worse
and worse all the time by loafing, sleeping, and
eating. But you, perhaps, think that it is a trifling
wrong when anyone makes another man worse.
And yet is it not right to keep away from such a
man above all as the deadliest and most
treacherous of enemies?"

DECEMBER 12

Diogenes Laertius – Book 2.77

When his servant was carrying money and found

the load too heavy, Aristippus cried, "Pour away the greater part, and carry no more than you can manage." […] Being once on a voyage, as soon as he discovered the vessel to be manned by pirates, he took out his money and began to count it, and then, as if by inadvertence, he let the money fall into the sea, and naturally broke out into lamentation. Another version of the story attributes to him the further remark that it was better for the money to perish on account of Aristippus than for Aristippus to perish on account of the money.

DECEMBER 13

Diogenes Laertius – Book 2.76

When Charondas[79] (or, as others say, Phaedo) inquired, "Who is this who reeks with unguents?" he replied, "It is I, unlucky soul, and the still more unlucky Persian king. But, as none of the other animals are at any disadvantage on that account, consider whether it be not the same with man. Confound the effeminates who spoil for us the use of good perfume."

DECEMBER 14

Diogenes Laertius – Book 2.68

---

[79] A celebrated lawgiver of Catania in Sicily

Being asked what he had gained from philosophy, [Aristippus] replied, "The ability to feel at ease in any society." [...] Being once asked what advantage philosophers have, he replied, "should all laws be repealed, we shall go on living as we do now."

DECEMBER 15

Athenaeus – Deipnosophistae Book 12

Accordingly, when he was assigned a very mean place at a banquet by Dionysius, he endured it patiently; and when Dionysius asked him what he thought of his present place, in comparison of his yesterday's seat, he said, "That the one was much the same as the other; for that one," says he, "is a mean seat today, because it is deprived of me; but it was yesterday the most respectable seat in the room, owing to me: and this one today has become respectable, because of my presence in it; but yesterday it was an inglorious seat, as I was not present in it." And in another place [the chronicler] says - "Aristippus, being ducked with water by Dionysius' servants, and being ridiculed by Antiphon[80] for bearing it patiently, said, "But suppose I had been out fishing, and got wet, was I to have left my employment, and come away?""

---

[80] The earliest of the ten Attic orators, and an important figure in fifth-century Athenian political and intellectual life.

DECEMBER 16

Diogenes Laertius – Book 2.80

To the critic who censured him for leaving
Socrates to go to Dionysius, [Aristippus'] rejoinder
was, "Yes, but I came to Socrates for education
and to Dionysius for recreation." When he had
made some money by teaching, Socrates asked
him, "Where did you get so much?" to which he
replied, "Where you got so little."

DECEMBER 17

Suda – Alpha 3909

It is said that when his child was carrying money
and was burdened by the weight [Aristippus] said,
"Then cast off what's weighing you down." When
he was being plotted against on a voyage he cast
into the sea the things on account of which he was
being conveyed. "For," he said, "the loss is my
salvation."

DECEMBER 18

Diogenes Laertius – Book 2.66

[Aristippus] was capable of adapting himself to
place, time and person, and of playing his part
appropriately under whatever circumstances.
Hence he found more favour than anybody else
with Dionysius, because he could always turn the

situation to good account. He derived pleasure from what was present, and did not toil to procure the enjoyment of something not present. Hence Diogenes called him the king's poodle. Timon[81], too, sneered at him for luxury in these words: Such was the delicate nature of Aristippus, who groped after error by touch.

DECEMBER 19

Diogenes Laertius – Book 2.81

[Aristippus] received a sum of money from Dionysius at the same time that Plato carried off a book and, when he was twitted with this, his reply was,, "Well, I want money, Plato wants books." Someone asked him why he let himself be refuted by Dionysius. "For the same reason," said he, "as the others refute him."

DECEMBER 20

Diogenes Laertius – Book 2.74

To the accusation that, although [Aristippus] was a pupil of Socrates, he took fees, his rejoinder was, "Most certainly I do, for Socrates, too, when certain people sent him corn and wine, used to take a little and return all the rest; and he had the

---

[81] A Greek Pyrrhonist philosopher, a pupil of Pyrrho, and a celebrated writer of satirical poems called Silloi.

foremost men in Athens for his stewards, whereas
mine is my slave Eutychides[82]."

DECEMBER 21

Diogenes Laertius – Book 2.71

An advocate, having pleaded for [Aristippus] and
won the case, thereupon put the question, "What
good did Socrates do you?" "Thus much," was the
reply, "that what you said of me in your speech
was true."

DECEMBER 22

Plutarch – On Curiosity 2

And Aristippus, meeting Ischomachus[83] at the
Olympic games, asked him what those notions
were with which Socrates had so powerfully
charmed the minds of his young scholars; upon
the slight information whereof, he was so
passionately inflamed with a desire of going to
Athens, that he grew pale and lean, and almost
languished till he came to drink of the fountain
itself, and had been acquainted with the person of
Socrates, and more fully learned that philosophy
of his, the design of which was to teach men how
to discover their own ills and apply proper
remedies to them.

---

[82] Eutychides means "good luck".
[83] A follower of Socrates

DECEMBER 23

Diogenes Laertius – Book 2.76-77

Polyxenus the [travelling] sophist once paid
[Aristippus] a visit and, after having seen ladies
present and expensive entertainment, reproached
him with it later. After an interval Aristippus asked
him, "Can you join us today?" On the other
accepting the invitation, Aristippus inquired,
"Why, then, did you find fault? For you appear to
blame the cost and not the entertainment."

DECEMBER 24

Plutarch – On the Virtues and Fortunes of
Alexander the Great, 8

It is a strange thing; we applaud Socratic
Aristippus, because, being sometimes clad in a
poor threadbare cloak, sometimes in a Milesian
robe[84], he kept a decency in both.

DECEMBER 25

Diogenes Laertius – Book 2.67

Hence the [the following] remark, "[Aristippus]
alone is endowed with the gift to flaunt in robes
or go in rags."

---

[84] Al luxurious type of robe, probably made with purple, the royal
color.

DECEMBER 26

Suda – Alpha 3909

And he came to Dionysius the tyrant of Sicily and
won the drinking and led the dance for the others
and put on purple clothes. But Plato, when the
robe was brought to [Aristippus], said some
iambics of Euripides: "I would not put on
feminine clothes, having been born male, and
from a male line." Aristippus took it and said with
a laugh [some lines] of the same poet: "for the
moderate mind will not be corrupted in Bacchic
revelries."

DECEMBER 27

Diogenes Laertius – Book 2.76

Being asked how Socrates died, [Aristippus]
answered, "As I would wish to die myself."

DECEMBER 28

Plutarch – Life of Dion 19.7

Thereupon Aristippus, jesting with the rest of the
philosophers, said that he himself also could
predict something strange. And when they
besought him to tell what it was, "Well, then,"
said he, "I predict that before long Plato and
Dionysius will become enemies."

DECEMBER 29

Aelian, – Varia Historia Book 14.6. – Aristippus
his opinion concerning cheerfulness.

Aristippus by strong arguments advised that we
should not be anxious about things past or future;
arguing, that not to be troubled at such things, is a
sign of a constant clear spirit. He also advised to
take care only for the present day, and in that day,
only of the present part, wherein something was
done or thought; for he said, the present only is in
our power, not the past or future; the one being
gone, the other uncertain whether ever it will
come.

DECEMBER 30

Athenaeus – Book 8

Why, even Aristippus the Socratic was a fish-eater,
and when reproached on one occasion by Plato
for his love of dainties, — but here is what the
Delphian writes: "When Plato criticized Aristippus
for buying so many fish, he replied that he had
bought them for only fourpence. To this Plato
said that he would have bought them himself at
that price, whereupon Aristippus said: "You see,
Plato! It isn"t I who am a fish-lover, but you who
are a money-lover."

DECEMBER 31

Diogenes Laertius – Book 2.68

Being reproached for his extravagance,
[Aristippus] said, "If it were wrong to be
extravagant, it would not be in vogue at the
festivals of the gods."

Printed in Great Britain
by Amazon

43533281R00108